THE INTERNET SEARCHER'S HANDBOOK

LOCATING
INFORMATION
PEOPLE
& SOFTWARE

Second Edition

Peter Morville, Louis Rosenfeld, and Joseph Janes

Second edition revised by GraceAnne A. DeCandido

NEAL-SCHUMAN NETGUIDE SERIES

Neal-Schuman Publishers, Inc.
New York   London

LSL
PROF
ZA
4201
.M67
1999

Published by Neal-Schuman Publishers, Inc.
100 Varick Street
New York, NY 10013

Copyright © 1999 by Neal-Schuman Publishers, Inc.
All rights reserved.
Printed and bound in the United States of America.

The paper used in this publication meets the minimum requirements of American National Standard for Information Sciences—Permanence of Paper for Printed Library Materials, ANSI Z39.48–1992.◯

Library of Congress Cataloging-in-Publication Data

Morville, Peter.
    The Internet searcher's handbook : locating information, people, and software / Peter Morville, Louis B. Rosenfeld, and Joseph Janes.
— 2nd ed. / rev. by GraceAnne A. DeCandido.
    p. cm. — (Neal-Schuman netguide series)
    ISBN 1–55570–359–3
    1. Internet searching. I. Rosenfeld, Louis B. II. Janes, Joseph. III. DeCandido, GraceAnne A. IV. Title. V. Series.
ZA4201.M67 1999
025.04—dc21
                                    99–38213
                                        CIP

Contents

Figures

Foreword

Richard Wiggins, Publisher, *InternetBuzz.com*

Brewster Kahle, the inventor of a pioneering Internet indexing and search mechanism called WAIS, once told a story about an Internet demonstration he gave at San Francisco's science museum, the Exploratorium. A variety of young people tried their hand at surfing the Internet, trying to find the specific things they wanted to learn more about. Then, one boy said, "I'd like to ask the Internet a question."

Kahle explained to the young man that, sadly, the Internet isn't that sort of critter. First off, there isn't any one place on the Internet to which you should present your question; you have to pick a particular information resource, then submit your query to that service, using the search language that facility expects. But wouldn't it be nice, Kahle wondered, if indeed users could simply ask the Internet a question and expect a reasonable answer?

That sort of simple model has been the dream of computer users as long as we've had online systems. Shouldn't we be able to ask the Internet all sorts of questions?

- What is the population of Senegal?
- What is the e-mail address for the admissions office at Auburn University?
- How did Congressman Ehlers vote on the communications decency bill last month?
- What books did C. S. Lewis write?

- Where did Governor George Bush attend college?
- What television programs are dedicated to Internet topics?
- Give me a list of bed-and-breakfasts in Saugatuck, Michigan.

These are all questions for which one can find answers on the Internet. Unfortunately, though, we can't just present these questions to a single, all-encompassing Internet interface and get the answers we're looking for. As a global network of networks, the Internet has far too many information resources, and far too diverse a set of information publishing tools, for things to be that simple.

Fictional computer systems would have no problem handling our example questions. A *Star Trek* character would simply say "computer" and ask any of these questions, and the machine would reply with the answer desired, delivered promptly and with smooth, modulated inflection. No computer today is that friendly and helpful, but a number of visionaries believe the day will soon arrive when online systems will achieve that level of responsiveness to our needs.

In fact, vendors of information technology software have tried for years to implement such systems. Ten years ago the goal was to devise "natural language" query mechanisms that sat atop existing databases. More recently, we've heard that the answer is an "information agent"—a tool that roams the Net, monitoring, gathering, filtering, and presenting information on our behalf. Numerous start-up companies say they'll win the race. Some of us believe that information agents have been oversold, and that we're a long way from carrying out productive voice conversations with our online systems.

In the meantime, we have to live in today's world. There are some analogies between how you find what you want on the Internet and how you find things in a traditional library. You wouldn't walk into a bricks-and-mortar library and, standing in the vestibule, begin shouting your question, expecting answers to flow forth from the building itself. From our early school days onward, we're taught how to exploit the standard reference resources of the library: when to go to the *Readers' Guide to Periodical Literature*, when to explore the *Encyclopaedia Britannica*, when to consult an unabridged dictionary, when to search the catalog (these days probably an online catalog, not a card catalog), and when to ask a reference librarian for assistance.

Similarly, when you want to find something on the Internet, you need some understanding of the standard reference materials and catalogs at your disposal. You also have to phrase the question appropriately for the catalog you're trying to consult.

In 1898 Halsey William Wilson found that his job as a bookseller was too complicated: keeping up with all the titles he might want for his inventory meant reading through numerous publishers' catalogs. He decided to create a single, *unified* catalog, which he christened the *Cumulative Book Index*. Today the H. W. Wilson Company remains an important vendor of library indexes. (You can read more about this story on the World Wide Web at *www.hwwilson.com/history.html*.)

In 1993 one of the authors of the first edition of this book, Lou Rosenfeld, saw a need for a single place to find resources on the Internet. He established the Clearinghouse for Subject-Oriented Internet Resource Guides at the University of Michigan. His goal was to have librarians and other Internet scouts collaborate to build a high-quality compendium of bibliographies. Today, the clearinghouse is sponsored by Argus Associates (*http://argus-inc.com*). The managing editor of the clearinghouse, Peter Morville, is the primary author of the first edition of this text. Rosenfeld and Morville are now the principals of Argus Associates. Argus seeks to do for the Internet community what H. W. Wilson sought to do for the print publishing world at the turn of the last century: bring order to an inherently chaotic realm.

The people at Argus Associates are not alone in this fin de siècle quest, of course. The names of Internet index tools become watchwords of the popular lexicon: in the early 1990s Archie, then Veronica, then Yahoo, Webcrawler, and Lycos. Corresponding to many of these names are highly successful commercial enterprises. More recently, new players have taken the stage: AltaVista, Infoseek, Excite, and HotBot.

In the late 1990s we see search engines trying to define their identity, moving beyond simple keyword indexes into the realm of "portals"— that neologism for the *TV Guide* of the Internet that each aspires to be. Brewster Kahle himself has deployed Alexa, a surfing companion that helps you find sites based on their popularity. And newcomer AskJeeves (*www.askjeeves.com*) even offers a "knowledge base" that lets you ask questions in natural language. (Memo to Exploratorium: that kid may get what he wants someday soon!)

Some of your Internet expeditions will involve searches for answers to serious questions; other searches will be more whimsical. Sometimes you won't really be searching at all, but rather browsing casually through information sources. (This is why even major research libraries usually offer browsing stacks.) Some people enjoy spending time skimming through dictionaries or encyclopedias, but those reading sessions are enjoyable only if you understand the landscape of the document you're reading. This book will help you understand the landscape of the Internet, so that you will find peripatetic browsing of the Net enjoyable and even serendipitous.

The Internet Searcher's Handbook, 2nd edition, will be uniquely useful because its authors are not just toolsmiths, but also scholars in the field of library science. Their discussion brings the singular insights of people who have helped advance the state of Internet catalogs from the perspective of library and information sciences. If the Internet is a virtual library, this book is your guided tour of the reference department and the catalog.

We eagerly await a new millennium and a new era in online information retrieval, the day when that boy can "ask the Internet a question" and get the answers he needs. In the meantime, let this book be your guide to the reality of resource discovery on today's Internet. Whether your goal is casual browsing or purposeful searching, your voyages will yield more fruit as a result.

Preface

Listening to television commentators hawking the Internet's many glories, it would be easy to believe that the Internet is a veritable shimmering ocean of digital information filled with stock reports, professional journals, image databases, and other wonders previously only available in the world's largest libraries. Even if one reads just a little bit, much of what is written about the Internet gives credance to the myth that powerful search tools are available to put that global network of information a mere mouse-click away.

Yet when Internet users begin to fish their first facts out of the Internet's murky depths, they soon find themselves lost in complex mazes of hypertext links, confusing search tools, and countless numbers of low-quality resources. In short, many Internet users soon find themselves "drowning in information" and ensnared in nets of "finding tools."

While it is true that since the first edition of this book was published in 1996 there are more—and much better-designed—search tools available, most of these tools have poor documentation and many Internet searchers still do not know that each tool serves a slightly different purpose. Thus, like its predecessor, this second edition of *The Internet Searcher's Handbook: Locating People, Information, and Software* is intended to provide an understanding of the principles of Internet searching and a detailed knowledge of currently available search tools.

With this aim in mind, *The Internet Searcher's Handbook* is divided into ten chapters. While each chapter was written to stand alone, the book is organized to serve as a comprehensive introduction to Internet information retrieval. Chapter One describes the Internet environment, provides a working vocabulary for the fundamentals of searching the Internet, defines types of search features, and provides tried-and-true searching tips. Chapter Two illustrates how to use the Web to answer reference questions and provides an overview of different types of informational sites on the Web. Chapter Three deconstructs the mysteries of metadata, explaining what it is and how it helps the everyday searcher. Chapter Four introduces searchers to bots, spiders, newsbots, chatterbots, and linkbots—all the creatures that roam the Web and (for the most part) make it easier to navigate. Chapter Five outlines how to use the Internet for conducting in-depth research and explores the fundamentals of Internet resource guides. Chapter Six provides an introduction to and tips for using online communities as information sources.

Chapters Seven, Eight, and Nine respectively provide in-depth information on virtual libraries, Internet directories, and Internet search tools. While there is significant overlap in the characteristics and uses of these tools, the distinctions between them are important to keep in mind. *Virtual libraries*, or "value-added collections of Internet resources," are the closest net-based equivalent to traditional libraries. By identifying, selecting, organizing, describing, and evaluating resources, "digital librarians" or "cybrarians" have created collections of pointers to valuable information sources. *Internet directories*, or "collections of resources maintained by the global Internet community," are the most comprehensive and popular of today's Internet tool set. Directories provide an organizational hierarchy that facilitates browsing and often complement their subject trees with a search interface. *Internet search tools* constitute the richest and most diverse of these three categories. Users interact with search tools via query interfaces that range from the simple to the sophisticated to aid users in finding information, software, people, and communities. This edition of *The Internet Searcher's Handbook* covers five virtual libraries, three Internet directories, and eight major search tools. The title, URL, purposes, searching tips, strengths, and weaknesses of each of these resources are provided. Sample searches are also included to illustrate when and how to effectively use the tool. Chapter Ten first provides an overview of Web rings and geographic information systems (GIS) and then sums up current searching needs while not quite daring to predict future search tool developments.

It is inevitable that the tools and resources described in these pages will become dated. Today's tools will evolve, move to new locations, or even cease to exist. New tools will be developed to take their places. This book is static; its subject, the Internet, is highly dynamic. For this reason, the authors have developed two Web sites to accompany this book. Lou Rosenfeld and Peter Morville maintain *The Internet Searching Center* (*www.clearinghouse.net/searching/index.html*), which provides quick access to all three types of searching resources covered in this book. GraceAnne DeCandido has developed an *Internet Searcher's Handbook Web Page* (*www.neal-schuman.com/ish.html*) featuring links organized in the order they are discussed within these pages. As URLs shift, these links will be updated so readers can locate and use the resources described quickly and painlessly. Armed with the narrative descriptions in these pages and these two online guides, the authors hope their readers will find Internet searching both less frustrating and more productive.

Acknowledgments

The authors and the publisher thank the following for giving permission to reprint screens from their Web sites in the following figures.

Figure 2–1 Reprinted with permission from *http://www.searchengine watch.com*. Copyright 1999 Internet.com Corporation. All rights reserved.

Figures 2–2 and 2–3 Copyright and used with permission of Whatis.com Inc. (*http://whatis.com*).

Figures 2–4 and 2–5 Virtual Reference Desk, a project of the ERIC Clearinghouse on Information & Technology and the National Library of Education with support from the Office of Science and Technology.

Figures 2–6, 2–7, and 5–5 courtesy of Deja.com™.

Figure 3–1 Reprinted with the permission of the New York Public Library Shomburg Collection.

Figure 3–2 Reprinted with permission from the University of Virginia.

Figures 4–1, 7–5, 7–6, and 9–3. Excite, the Excite Logo, and the Magellan Logo are trademarks and/or service marks of Excite, Inc., a subsidiary of At Home Corporation and may be registered in various jurisdictions. Excite and Magellan displays copyright 1995–1999 Excite, Inc.

Figures 5–1, 7–1, and 7–2 Reprinted with the permission of Argus Clearinghouse.

Figures 5–3 and 9–6 © 1999 Lycos, Inc. Lycos® is a registered trademark of Carnegie Mellon University. All rights reserved.

Figures 5–4 and 9–14 Reprinted with permission from Publicly Available Mailing Lists.

Figures 7–3 and 7–4 Copyright 1999 The Internet Library *http://ipl.org.*

Figure 7–7 Reprinted with permission from World Wide Web Virtual Library.

Figure 7–8 Used with permission from the Beer Info Source.

Figures 7–9 and 7–10 Reprinted with permission from About.com.Inc. About.com can be found on the Web at *www.about.com.*

Figures 8–1 and 8–2 Copyright © 1993–1999 AHN Partners, L. P. All rights reserved.

Figures 8–5 and 8–6 Copyright © 1999. All rights reserved. Maintained by Carole Leita: *cleita@sunsite.berkeley.edu.* Supported in part by Federal Library Services and Technology Act funding, administered by the California State Library.

Figure 9–1 The AltaVista logo brand and the Search Engine Content are copyright and trademarks of AltaVista Company. Used with permission.

Figure 9–2 Copyright 1996–1999, Ask Jeeves, Inc., Berkeley, California, all rights reserved. "Ask Jeeves," "Ask.com" and the Ask Jeeves logo are service marks of Ask Jeeves, Inc. Patent Pending.

Figure 9–4 © 1994–99 Wired Digital Inc. All rights Reserved.

Figure 9–5 Reprinted by permission. Infoseek, Ultraseek, Ultraseek Server are trademarks of Infoseek Corporation which may be registered in certain jurisdictions. Other trademarks shown are trademarks of their respective owners. Copyright © 1994–1999 Infoseek Corporation. All rights reserved. GO Network is a trademark of Disney Enterprises, Inc. 1998–1999, Infoseek Corporations authorized licensee.

Figure 9–7 Reprinted with permission of Northern Light.

Figure 9–8 Reprinted with permission. Google is a trademark of Google Inc.

Figure 9–9 Reprinted with the express permission of Go2Net, Inc.

Figure 9–10 Reprinted with permission of Inter-Links Opening Page

Figure 9–11 Reprinted with permission from InferenceFind.

Figure 9–12 Opening page for FAQ Archives at University of Utrecht reprinted with permission.

Figure 9–14 Reprinted with permission from Kovacs Consulting Internet & World Wide Web Training.

Figure 10–1 Reprinted with permission from WebRing, Inc., a division of Yahoo! Inc.

Figure 10–2 The New York State GIS Clearinghouse is a service of the New York State Office for Technology and is hosted by the New York State Library.

Figure 10–3 Library Selection Criteria for WWW Resources reprinted with permission.

Chapter One

Fundamentals of Searching Digital Resources

Joseph Janes

For the introductory chapter of the first edition of this book, I wrote a little story about what people often went through in discovering the Internet: big media hype and overblown expectations, initial excitement of discovery of some really cool stuff, and eventual disillusionment about too much stuff, too much crap, and the difficulty of finding anything really good. I wrote that chapter not so long ago in real time, but in Web time the chapter is Paleozoic. It actually contains the sentence "Gophers aren't maintained."

Parts of that chapter would seem positively quaint now if they weren't so telling. A lot of what I wrote is pointless because the technology has moved so quickly, but a lot still holds up, in part because the technology hasn't moved that far. There is still quite a bit of good stuff on the Web and a lot of stuff that's not so good, and it can still be very difficult to find that good stuff.

The popular-media story has changed somewhat. It still seems as though we're being told that the entire human record is on the Internet (how many ads with URLs have you seen today?), and that if you just choose the correct service (that is, search engine, portal, or directory), you can find what you're looking for, no muss no fuss. Somehow it also seems that 90 percent or so of the Net is porn (and therefore we have to have filters or laws to protect us from our baser natures, but that's a matter for another book). It's not true, of course, but it does pervade our thinking about the Internet.

I

In this chapter, I want to present an overview of networked informa- tion resources and their environment, give some words of wisdom about search strategy and technique, as well as provide some advice about how to look for stuff effectively. Keep in mind, though, that by the time you read this, many things will have changed. I'll focus less on specific ser- vices or features and more on ideas and strategies. Who knows what will have happened by the time the third edition is written?

THE BIG PICTURE: NETWORKED INFORMATION RESOURCES

The range of information resources available in digital formats, either exclusively, primarily, or as companion versions of print resources, con- tinues to grow daily. We are now accustomed to library catalogs in digi- tal form, often incorporating access to other tools as well (journal indexes, for example). Similarly, access to databases via commercial vendors and CD-ROMs is commonplace.

New genres of resources have arisen in the distributed networked en- vironment, and many of these resources have no print analogs or they share little with the more stable and familiar electronic sources. To be able to use these new sources, search them, and decide when they might be most appropriate, it is important to understand something about their nature and how they differ from their ancestors.

The Environment: Distributed and Dynamic

The two most important things to understand about the networked world are that it is a *distributed* environment and it is a *dynamic* environment. These two different but related characteristics define this world and help you to know how best to use it and live in it.

"Distributed," means that the environment has no center, no overall authority, no tangible sense of coherence. Thousands upon thousands of computers are connected to the Internet, and each of them has the capability to make information resources available, instantly and in most cases free of charge, to a global audience in the millions. Nobody can stop you, once you're connected, from putting up whatever you like. Clearly this unprecedented freedom to publish and communicate ideas has enormous potential for intellectual exchange and knowledge sharing.

Furthermore, this environment is dynamic. Each of these resources can change by the second. New resources arise daily; others move or become unavailable for one reason or another. Most are not updated that rapidly (and indeed, many are never updated, raising altogether different problems), but the potential for nearly instantaneous responsiveness and creativity is exciting.

It's also a pain in the neck. Since there are virtually no controls over who can put what out there, things change continually, and, since there are no standards for what librarians think of as intellectual control (cataloging, indexing, organization, and so forth), it's a mess. It can be fun and challenging and occasionally enlightening to simply wander around, surfing through the contours of the Net, coming across all sorts of new and different things. But there's also a lot of worthless, idiosyncratic garbage, and finding anything good (or indeed anything at all) on a particular topic can be difficult at best. Most of the things that we take for granted in the world of books, libraries, and commercial information products exist on the Net in crude, simplistic forms or not at all.

Net Resources versus Standard Commercial Resources

Many of the differences we can identify between Net and standard commercial sources stem from the lack of standards in the networked world. The freedom and flexibility offered by the Net have not yet given way or forced the development of standard information structures, search facilities, styles, and so on. There is a growing appreciation among many people who create and use Net resources that such things are important, and some tentative steps have been taken (largely in the realm of metadata, with such ideas as the Dublin Core, which is discussed in Chapter Three), but little has yet become widely accepted or established.

Four characteristics of networked resources are worth noting in more detail:

- **Dynamism:** Although mentioned above, it's worth restating that we are not used to books or articles or other print resources that change overnight. To be sure, databases are continually updated and new editions are common, but the nature of these changes is less dramatic than what is found on the Net. It is not unusual, on a typical day of working with networked resources, to find that one has changed its address (and, with luck, has left a link leading you to the new location), another has been updated and thus the interface has changed, a third is gone entirely because its creator has graduated from college and no longer maintains it, and a new one has come up with a great deal of potentially interesting material. Not every resource changes every day, but the degree and speed of change on the network are often disorienting.
- **Quality, Review, Authority:** An article does not get published in

the *New England Journal of Medicine* or any other scholarly journal without undergoing a rigorous process of peer review and approval. Books do not get published by Random House or major houses without being edited both in content and style. Entries are not added to databases like Sociological Abstracts without being checked for conformity with indexing and other style policies. Such checks on style, grammar, authority, and quality have not been widely implemented in the networked world. Some scholarly journals do appear in electronic form with the same treatment as printed journals, and a few attempts have been made to apply such standards to other resources, but in general it is *caveat lector*—let the reader beware. Many people are aware of the need of such procedures to make the Net an attractive and worthwhile medium for serious communication and knowledge sharing, but the lack of central authority and consensus have so far prevented much from taking hold.

- **Currency:** Despite the fact that networked resources can be updated with ease, many aren't regularly updated. It is easy to create a resource and even easier to leave it alone once it is up. Maintaining, updating, and developing networked resources is a continual challenge, and one that not all creators meet successfully. Again, a great many resources are up-to-date and current, and thus very useful. For other resources, continual updating may not be necessary, but lack of updating can be a problem in some cases.

- **Functionality:** In addition, these resources often have features and functions that traditional print resources do not. Some resources are fairly pedestrian: the ability to search in new ways (say, in quotation fields of the *Oxford English Dictionary* or in full text of the *Encyclopaedia Britannica*) is really just a simple matter once a resource is digital. Other resources, however, take advantage of the hypertextual environment of the Web—Parliamentary and Presidential Elections around the World (*www.agora.stm.it/elections/election.htm*), for example, is not only a good repository of information but it also links to Web sites from national parliaments, governments, and even political parties and election coverage. Still other resources make use of the cooperative nature of the Web world. The Internet Movie Database (*http://us.imdb.com*), for example, is maintained in part by the participation of hundreds of movie nuts around the world and is thus probably the finest resource on film today.

> ### Three Major Categories of Search Tools on the Net
>
> 1. Virtual libraries or catalogs (the Argus Clearinghouse, the Internet Public Library)
>
> 2. Internet directories (Yahoo)
>
> 3. Search engines (AltaVista, HotBot, Excite, Metacrawler)
>
> The first two categories are primarily browsing tools, although many incorporate search features; the third is primarily for specific searching. The terminology is pretty fluid, and it would not be unusual to find the same resource called by any of these three names. They tend to differ in the degree of consistency and coherence they provide, as well as in functionality, editorial control, and focus.

This, then, is the environment in which any searcher must operate in trying to identify potentially valuable information on the Net. It is not as completely hopeless as it may sound from this discussion. A number of tools have been developed to make finding things easier.

WORK THE SYSTEM: TECHNIQUE AND STRATEGIC TIPS

Broadly stated, there are three major categories of search tools on the Net: virtual libraries or catalogs (like the Argus Clearinghouse, the Internet Public Library), Internet directories (e.g., Yahoo), and search engines (e.g., AltaVista, HotBot, Excite, Metacrawler). The first two categories are primarily browsing tools, although many incorporate search features; the third is primarily for specific searching. The terminology is pretty fluid, and it would not be unusual to find the same resource called by any of these three names. They tend to differ in the degree of consistency and coherence they provide, as well as in functionality, editorial control, and focus.

When to Use What

Simply put, it's usually best to search for specific words and phrases and known items (if they have specific, unambiguous names), by using search engines (things like AltaVista, Lycos, Excite, HotBot). Searching is what they do, and they do it reasonably well. You have to be careful sometimes, because you can get a lot of junk, especially with common or ambiguous words. In addition, these search engines often lack features you'd like; not every one will let you know which databases they are searching.

You're better off using directories such as Yahoo when you want a number of things that are alike or on the same topic. I go to Yahoo primarily for this—looking more for categories than sites, and since they also have a search engine I use that rather than the now cumbersome and overloaded category system.

So, for example, if I were looking for the contents of the last meal before the execution of Ted Bundy, the serial murderer, I'd probably use a search engine, since his name is relatively unambiguous and the phrase *last meal* is pretty meaningful, too. On the other hand, if I were looking for good sites that talk about the television series *Babylon 5*, I'd go to Yahoo to see if there is a category on the show (there is), and explore what's in that category. As it turns out, there are lots of sites; Yahoo often provides little or no descriptive information and next to no evaluation, so that process can be tedious, but at least you have all the candidates in front of you.

Preparing to Search

As with any searches in the print or commercial digital domain, a search on the Net requires several steps of preparation: understanding the topic or topics of interest, extracting one or more concepts inherent in the question, identifying potentially useful terms that adequately represent those concepts, selecting possible resources and tools to use, and executing the search.

But of course, as we know, this preparation doesn't always happen. Many searches are the quick-and-dirty, take-no-prisoners type and most Net search services facilitate that sort of thing. There's nothing wrong with them, and we all do them, but if you're serious, you really ought to think about the search for just a moment before diving in headfirst.

Again, it is important to acknowledge the environment in which the search will take place. For example, since there are few standards of indexing, classification, or vocabulary control in networked resources, it is almost always impossible to use any controlled vocabularies or thesauri. Familiar tools such as the *Library of Congress Subject Headings* or the *Thesaurus of Psychological Index Terms* are of little help. Rather, colloquial expressions, slang, metaphorical uses of words, and nonstandard use of words are common on the Net, and may either obscure potentially useful resources or combine with content words (actual search terms) and thus produce lots more hits. (Witness what's happened to the word *spam*, which now not only means the meat-in-a-can we all know and love but also means unwanted e-mail. Searching for Spam™ recipes is now a more difficult proposition.) Furthermore, since much of what exists on the Net revolves around the Net itself and computing more generally, searching on words like *Internet*, *Net*, *computer*, *archive*, *software*, and so on is typically useless.

This all means that decision making on the part of the searcher becomes even more critical. In fact, many of these decisions are similar to those familiar to most librarians. What are the best resources to use in these circumstances, based on experience with the tools, coverage of various resources, features available for use, constraints of time and money, quality of the information, reputation of the source, and so on? The questions don't really change much. This sort of professional assessment of the environment and how best to work within it, though, becomes even more important in such a chaotic and dynamic climate.

SEARCH FEATURES

A number of features are available in most commercial or library systems that experienced (and not-so-experienced) searchers can use to refine or improve the quality of their searching. These features have evolved over the years as technologies have grown more sophisticated, and they require a substantial amount of preparation and work to implement. In this section, I'll discuss the more important of these features and see whether they can be used in the networked environment. In exploring these features, I'll use the example of looking for information about millennial cults.

Truncation

Many commercial systems support truncation, which allows the searcher to specify that documents must contain at least a particular character string. The truncation symbol may vary from one system to another, but it is often the question mark, the asterisk, the pound sign, or the percent sign. A search on **CULT?** in one system, for example, will produce all documents containing words that begin with *cult*, such as *cult*, *cults*, *cultist*, *cultism*, and so on. This broad search will probably gather most of the documents on cults in the database.

Truncation is a powerful tool, but it also has some obvious side effects, the most important of which is the problem of over-truncation (this search will also get us *cultivate*, *culture*, and so on). Indeed, some systems have several truncation commands, and an experienced searcher would probably choose (if the system allows) to search on **CULT? ?**, indicating a wish for only one additional character, rather than an arbitrary number.

Truncation is actually rather common in network-based tools, but it is not always obvious, may be called other things, and might even be invisible. For example, some search engines automatically truncate. Typing **CULT** will get you all the variants listed above automatically. You actually have to tell them *not* to truncate (by adding a period to the ends of words).

It's common for some simple search engines to ask if you wish to search for your words as complete words or as substrings. "Substring" is a term from computer science, and it means that the series of characters you ask for will occur somewhere in the word but not necessarily at the beginning. (Experienced searchers will recognize that this amounts to implicit left-hand and right-hand truncation.) So a substring search, for example, on **CULT** will produce even more false retrievals, such as *agriculture* and *horticulture*. Asking to search only complete words, in these systems, however, stops truncation altogether; there is often no middle ground.

Boolean Searching

In our example, the searcher wants documents that include not only the word *cult* in some form but also the word *millennium*. This search can easily be accomplished by using the Boolean operator AND. **MILLENNIUM AND CULT?** produces the set of documents containing both required words. The other two Boolean operators, OR (used to combine spelling variations, synonyms, and related words) and NOT (used to eliminate terms), may also be used. (A note: some engines require AND NOT, and some require all Boolean operators to be capitalized.)

In the Net world, another set of commands achieves similar aims. You can often use the plus sign (+) to specify that a word or phrase must be in retrieved documents (which is like an AND), and the minus sign (-) to specify that a word or phrase must not be in retrievals (like NOT). Thus, you might try **+MILLENNIUM +CULTS -CARTER** to get documents about these cults, but not those that mention Chris Carter, the creator of the television series *Millennium*.

Adjacency, Ranking, and Phrases

Experienced online searchers will know that they could do better than **MILLENNIUM AND CULT?** (which only requires that the two words be in the same document, whether they have anything to do with each other or not). Using proximity or adjacency operators, we can specify that these two words must appear next to each other, in this order, for a document to be retrieved. Asking for **MILLENNIUM(W)CULT?** would not retrieve documents that mention, for example, horticulture in one paragraph and the millennium bug in the next.

Many Internet search tools appear to provide this adjacency feature. They allow searchers to type words and phrases, and they magically produce retrievals. However, they really employ algorithms that look for the target words in documents and then calculate scores for each based on several factors: for example, how often the words occur, whether they occur early or late in documents or in titles, whether they occur close together, their overall frequency, and so on. Some of these formulas are quite complex, and they are almost always hidden from the user. So typing **MILLENNIUM CULTS,** for example, produces a ranked list of documents, largely on topic, but also ranging from sites about the television show *Millennium* to several software sites and the *National Geographic* site. These systems are quite powerful and they often produce good results, but it can be a bit disconcerting, especially to those experienced with commercial systems, not to be able to have more control over retrievals.

Although it provides fewer options than proximity operators, it is now common in Net searching to be able to specify that a search be conducted on a phrase (as opposed to ranking individual words). So you could type "**MILLENNIUM CULTS**"—using the quotation marks, as they are the usual way of specifying phrase searching—and usually retrieve only documents with that complete intact phrase.

AltaVista permits a version of proximity searching with the NEAR operator, which will retrieve documents where words are phrases are within five words of each other—beginning—but there's still quite a way to go for really precise searching.

Fields and Context

In commercial systems, there are a great many other commands at the searcher's disposal. I'll discuss only two more: the ability to search for words in particular fields of the document (such as the title, the abstract, the index terms) and the ability to focus a search based on the context of documents (say, only retrieving documents from particular years or in particular languages). One might see a search such as this:

(MILLENNI?("N)CULT? ?)/TI AND PY>=1998

which would look for variants of the phrase *millennium cults* or *millennial cults* in the title field of documents published in 1998 or later.

These capabilities are only now emerging on the Internet. It is likely that they will continue to arise as more time and effort are spent on developing search facilities, but at the moment, only a few rudimentary features of this sort are available. They often take the form of check boxes or fill-in fields, removing the need for users to remember a large or cumbersome set of commands.

The reason these capabilities are appearing slowly if at all is due to the amount of work required to make them available. Not only do the search engines need to be designed, but database indexes must be sophisticated enough to support searching words together, in specific fields. Documents must include tags about dates, languages, authorship, and other contextual information. Then there is the whole question of indexing, classification, and name authority, so common in familiar library systems, which is only now dawning on the Net world. There is clearly a long way to go to make these systems as reliable and powerful as those found in the commercial realm.

ADVICE FOR THE SEARCHLORN

Finally, let me offer a few pieces of advice that I think will be of assistance. Again, these tips are not specific to any particular service, but I find them to be helpful.

Use the Most Direct Approach

Search engines and directories are fine, and indeed useful in many situations. But you should always try to figure out the most direct line of search. In particular, think if you need to search at all. It may be possible to go directly to a Web site without searching. For example, if you were looking for information about the American Library Association, you might go to *www.ala.org*. Web sites like *www.whitehouse.gov*, *www.biography.com*, and *www.nytimes.com* are good examples of intuitive addresses.

Sometimes it takes a bit of guesswork (*www.amnesty.org* for Amnesty International, *www.nwa.com* for Northwest Airlines, *state.mi.us* for the State of Michigan), and you can go badly wrong (for example, *www.whitehouse.com*—which you should know is an explicit sexual site), but creative guesswork can often be an effective (and quick) technique.

Let Somebody Else Do the Work

Why search if somebody else has done the hard work for you? Use a resource like the Argus Clearinghouse (*www.clearinghouse.net*) or the Internet Public Library (*www.ipl.org*), which selects and organizes resources in categories and on particular topics.

Also, when searching in an area I know little about but in which there is a lot of information, I often try to find a site compiled by an expert (or at least by somebody with a lot of interest in the area and a lot of free time). Such sites not only provide access to a lot of information but they also provide a point of view, an organizational structure, background, additional information, and so on.

A variant of this strategy is to find a Usenet group, listserve, or Web ring in the area. Then look for a FAQ (frequently asked questions) list; and, if you don't find the answer there, post a question to the list and see if anyone answers.

Take Advantage of Full-Text Searching and Ranking

As professional searchers know, full-text searching is a double-edged sword. The ability to search the entire text of documents is powerful, but sometimes too powerful, and it opens the door to many problems of ambiguity, synonymy, metaphor, and just plain weird uses of words. (How many senses of the word *pitch* can you think of right now? Exactly.)

But you might as well take advantage of it. If you can think of a way to say something, there's always a chance that somebody else has thought of it too and, more to the point, has put up a Web site on it. If you're looking for information about numerical values assigned to the Greek alphabet, you could do worse than search on that phrase and see what happens.

Find a Favorite, But Don't Get Too Attached to It

It seems that most experienced Web searchers I know have a favorite search engine or service. They're never really happy with it all the time, but it makes life easier to have a single place to start and not have to think about it really hard.

On the other hand, part of the trick here is to know when not to start with your favorite. Knowing special features of other search engines or when to use a meta-searcher or directory can save time. Furthermore, be prepared to abandon your favorite when you feel it's not helping any more. Perhaps its interface has become too difficult to use, your results are suffering, or the database isn't being refreshed often enough. When it's over, it's over, and you should just move on.

Don't Be Afraid to Ask for Help, But Don't Expect Miracles

All of these sites have help screens, which vary in terms of actual help provided. None of them will tell you how a search engine works, because the methods they use are their competitive advantage, but at the very least they'll tell you what kinds of commands are available, provide suggestions on how to use them, and so on. Be sure to notice the differences between "regular" and "advanced" searching—they can be substantial and surprising. To use features such as field searching, Boolean operators, and so on, you may have to use the "advanced" searching options, but sometimes you give up "behind-the-scenes" functionality to do that, so be sure you know what you're doing.

In addition, there are sites—my favorite is Search Engine Watch (*www.searchenginewatch.com*)—that provide information on all search mechanisms, including comparison tests, tips on how to use the mechanisms effectively and tips on how to write your documents to get high scores (metatagging), and even gossip. (See Chapter Two for more detail about this site). Such sites can be very useful, especially in getting the big picture and knowing how things are changing.

WHAT WILL THIS CHAPTER LOOK LIKE IN THE THIRD EDITION OF THIS BOOK?

Good question. Much as I hate predictions, I think it's likely that as we proceed into an information environment that increasingly incorporates networked resources (but not to the exclusion of print and commercial digital stuff) we will see:

- More sophisticated searching techniques. I doubt it will ever be as sophisticated as Dialog or Lexis/Nexis technique, but it will get better.
- Services that are easy to use, which probably means lots of check boxes, with menus and options hidden to beginning searchers but available for experts.
- More value-added services, like the categories of human-selected "good sites" that we now see, and maybe context-sensitive automatic help or even human help (perhaps for a fee).
- Specialized search engines and services by subject area, population, language, and so on, to make it easier to find good stuff. Of course, finding those services will now become a challenge.
- Greater presence of libraries, librarians, and their perspective on information. Call this one a hopeful scenario for the future. OCLC's NetFirst database of Web resources is a good example of this emerging library presence. What librarians bring to the information world is of such value; I just hope we can find a way to incorporate their expertise and help people to realize its importance.

I reserve the right to be completely wrong about these predictions, and if I write the introductory chapter to the third edition, not to mention them at all.

Chapter Two

Using the Web to Answer Reference Questions

Sara Ryan

In the three years between the first and the second editions of this book, many more librarians have become sophisticated Internet searchers, and so have their users. A significant percentage of libraries have Web sites that are substantial repositories of useful information customized for specific patron communities. But the Internet continues to increase in complexity and disorder by the day, and the changes intended to make searching easier can instead make searchers even more confused and frustrated.

THE LAY OF THE LAND

A recent report estimated that the Web is now responsible for seventy-five percent of the traffic over the Internet ("The Nature of the Beast: Recent Traffic Measurements from an Internet Backbone," K. Claffy, G. Miller, and K. Thompson, paper presented at the Internet Society 1998 Annual Meeting, *www.caida.org/Papers/Inet98/*). David Plotnikoff noted in the *San Jose Mercury News* that "an alarming number of people confuse the Internet and the World Wide Web in conversation. The two are not one and the same. The two terms are not any more interchangeable than the words wine and Cabernet." ("The Internet, Web, History, and a Rant," October 16, 1998, *www.mercurycenter.com/columnists/plotnikoff/docs/dp101898.htm*). As Plotnikoff explains, the Web is a subset of the traffic on the overall Internet, which also includes e-mail and

Usenet news, among other applications. In this chapter, I will concentrate on ways to search the Web, but will also describe a few tools that allow you to search non-Web-based Internet content. Answering "stumpers," an important Internet function, is discussed in Chapter Six.

The Web has definitely become the dominant Internet application. It has grown exponentially in the past few years, and a substantial portion of this growth is in commercial sites. Among the many commercial entities that are now absolutely guaranteed to have Web sites are big-budget movies, businesses that want to be perceived as technologically savvy and forward-thinking, musical groups with any kind of following at all, and publishers of traditional print media. Commercial Web sites are so ubiquitous that the two dominant Web browsers, Netscape and Internet Explorer, allow the user simply to type a word into their Location/Address box, and the browser will insert *www* as a prefix and *.com* as a suffix. When I teach kids about evaluating Web sites, and tell them that Web site addresses are called URLs, for Uniform Resource Locator, they frequently ask, "You mean the .com thing?" They aren't even aware that there are any other types of sites.

Internet Domains

The following section is adapted from handouts produced for the Multnomah County Library School Corps to teach students and teachers about evaluating the accuracy of information from the Web. It is an overview of the different types of Internet domains and the kinds of information likely to be found on pages within each one.

.COM

The extension .com signifies a commercial site: a site that a company owns. Sometimes the company is one that provides Internet services, like America Online. The Web pages of people who subscribe to America Online will include *aol.com* because those people are buying Web space from America Online. So a .com site can be the actual Web site of a company, or it can be Web space that a company is selling to people.

Commercial sites are often difficult to evaluate because, more and more frequently, companies include educational information on portions of their sites. For instance, the Duracell site includes a feature on the history of batteries that explains the chemistry involved in making a battery. And all librarians who use the Web to answer reference questions are familiar with the phenomenon of the dedicated hobbyists who buy space from Internet Service Providers (ISPs) to present an exhaustive amount of information on whatever their passion happens to be. In many cases, those hobbyists are conscientious about providing citations for the information sources they used while compiling their Web site on, say, the history of dachshund breeding. In some cases, however, they are not.

.EDU

If you see *.edu*, you know that the site is an educational site from a college or university. Usually, you'd think this would mean that the site has good information. But sometimes, colleges and universities give Web space to students, and the students may or may not check their facts when they put up information.

K12

When *K12* appears in the URL, it means that the site comes from a primary or secondary school. Sometimes teachers make pages, sometimes students do. Many teachers put student projects on part of their school's Web sites.

.ORG

If you see *.org*, you know that the site comes from a nonprofit organization. If you use information from a nonprofit organization's site, think about the organization's agenda and how it is likely to influence the way they present information. For instance, if you are researching drugs, you will find substantially different points of view presented at the Campaign for a Drug-Free America and NORML: the National Organization for the Reform of Marijuana Laws. Just as when you are using print publications to do research, you need to keep in mind that the organization providing the information may want to influence you to agree with their perspective on the topic at hand.

.GOV

Sites with *.gov* in the address are produced by some government agency, most often at the federal level, more rarely by other levels of government.

.MIL

A *.mil* site is produced by some agency within the United States military.

.NET

The *.net* extension means that the site has something to do with providing Internet-related service. Sometimes ISPs will have *.net* as part of their addresses, although they might also be *.com*.

Country Codes

These guidelines are all good for sites within the United States. Sites outside the United States may have their own two- or three-letter country codes: for example, the United Kingdom's code is *.uk*, and a commercial site from the United Kingdom would have *.com.uk* as part of its address. (Note they may also have *.com*, etc., without the country code, depending on their ISP.) You can find a list of country codes at *www.iana.org/country-codes.txt*.

The country code system has some amusing side effects. Devotees of Yiddish are eager to get Web space on servers in the South Pacific nation of Niue because the country's domain name (*.nu*) is a Yiddish word. And residents of Tuvalu, nine small islands scattered over 500,000 miles of the western Pacific just south of the equator, stand to make a lot of money selling Web space with their nation's domain name: *.tv*.

There are also some new domain names in the works, because many people believe that the current system makes Web addresses too difficult to understand for the average user. The new domain names include *.shop* (for companies selling goods over the Web) and *.nom* (for personal home pages), as well as *.arts* and *.rec* (for arts-oriented and recreational material respectively).

Tilde (~)

If you see a tilde (~) in the address, you'll know that an individual created the page. Make sure sources are cited if you're considering using this information to answer a reference question. Use your judgment, however: universities offer Web space to their faculty members as well as to their students, and it's probably all right if a prominent researcher doesn't cite sources on a Web page when discussing the topic of his or her own expertise.

KNOWING WHAT TO LOOK FOR

If you're going to use the Web to answer reference questions, it's important to know the kinds of questions it is best suited to answer. Here is a brief overview of the subjects that you're likely to find good information about on the Web.

- **Computers and the people who use them.** The Web is a great source of information about the Web! You will find multiple sites about Web design; HTML, DHTML, SGML, and XML standards;

What Can You Find on the Web?

It's fairly easy to find good information on the Web about:

- Computers and the people who use them
- Current events
- Opinions from every part of the spectrum
- Popular culture and entertainment

It is much rarer to find good information on the Web in areas like these:

- Detailed biographies
- Obscure historical information

Don't assume it's there, and don't assume it's not.

Java Applets; and so on. More broadly, you will also find hardware and software specifications, tutorials, product and price information from computer companies, freeware and shareware programs to download, and a zillion sites that offer strategies for winning one computer game or another.

- **Current events**. All the major news providers have substantial sites, most of which are updated several times daily. For instance, within hours of the *Starr Report* being published online, it was available from more sites than you could shake a stained blue dress at. There are also multiple Web sources for stock quotes, sports scores, and other topics of pressing interest but ephemeral nature.

- **Opinions**. I'm not being facetious. The Internet is, among many other things, a vast conglomeration of opinions, some informed, some uninformed. Survey researchers are just beginning to use those opinions seriously to study the populations on the Internet. But obviously, having access to a huge number of wildly divergent opinions about any given subject is both a blessing and a curse for the information seeker.

- **Popular culture and entertainment**. If someone loved it as a child, or if someone can't go a Tuesday night without watching it now, there's information about it on the Internet. Television shows and movies are reviewed, comic books and toys are idolized and sold, stars are idolized and/or hated—and in either case, their pictures are scanned. For instance, supermodel Cindy Crawford finally authorized the creation of a site in her honor, cindy.com, after learning how many unauthorized sites about her were already on the Web.

The kinds of information unlikely to be found on the Web are more difficult to generalize about, because there are always exceptions. But here are two types of information that you probably will not find on the Web.

- **Detailed biographies**. The Web is a great place for one-screen summaries of people's lives. Any number of sites will tell you when and where Famous Person X was born, how X achieved notoriety, and when and where X died. But you are extremely unlikely to find any sites that have the depth and comprehensiveness of a print biography.
- **Detailed, obscure historical information**. You can find lots of sites that provide outlines of historical periods. But if you're trying to find out anything about, say, the details of a 17th-century peasant rebellion in Wales, you're probably not going to find it on the Web. (Unless, of course, the preeminent researcher on the topic has decided to make her research available, which is always a possibility, but not a high probability.)

Did I mention details? One problem with the Web is that many sites cater to people with short attention spans. There's enormous breadth of information, but not much depth.

It used to be that you couldn't ever find proprietary information on the Web. But now, database producers often offer free trial subscriptions to their information, on the "your first fix is free" concept. The reasoning behind such offers is that people will become hooked on the information and then be willing to pay to continue to have access to it. But some Web commentators have pointed out that so many vendors are doing this that it would be theoretically possible to "surf" from one free trial subscription to the next, without ever having to purchase access.

A good rule of thumb for searching for any type of information on the Web is the following: *Don't assume it's there, and don't assume it's not.* Some of the things you would think are the most likely to be found on the Web simply aren't there, and vice versa. When in doubt, do a quick keyword search and see what you get: you may be surprised. And when you search for anything on the Web, always try to think of the most specific word or words that could describe what you're looking for.

WHAT WAS THAT MASKED SEARCH TOOL?

Way back when, maybe about a year ago, when you searched for information on the Web, two basic types of tools were available: search engines and subject directories.

Search engines use programs called "spiders" to visit Web sites and index their content. These index entries are then compiled into a large database. When you type keywords into a search engine, you search the contents of that database. Lycos, AltaVista, and HotBot are examples of search engines.

Subject directories are human-compiled collections of links to Web sites, frequently hierarchical, organized by topic. Many librarians have created subject directories as components of library Web sites.

The reason this distinction matters is that spider programs can't assess Web sites for authority, relevance, timeliness, or any of the other qualities that human information searchers typically value. So it used to be that you could recommend that searchers start out at a human-compiled subject directory, and only move on to a search engine if they didn't find anything relevant in the subject directory.

The first thing that complicated this simple distinction was that the Web's most popular subject directory, Yahoo, incorporated a search engine into its site early on in its development. So when you typed a keyword into Yahoo, you searched the contents of its human-compiled database the same way that you could search the contents of the spider-compiled databases of the search engines. Although this was a valuable development in some senses, it made the distinction between search engines and subject directories substantially more complicated to explain to the average user.

The next development was on the search engine side. Some bright programmers observed that people liked to search more than one engine, to feel more like they were getting all the Web had to offer (of course no search engine database comes close to indexing all the sites out there). They decided to make a new kind of search engine: the meta-engine. Meta-engines search the databases of several search engines at once, though they typically only return 10 to 50 sites from each engine. You can specify the number of seconds you want the meta-engine to search, which can sometimes speed up the search process. Examples of meta-search engines are Metacrawler and Google. (See Chapter Nine for descriptions of different search engines.)

Then, of course, many of the most prominent search engines observed Yahoo's huge success and decided to incorporate subject directories on

Once upon a time, **search engines** used "spiders" to search the Web and index its content. **Subject directories** were made by people, not programs, and organized by content. But then search engines and subject directories merged in interesting ways, blurring their distinct natures and metamorphosing into **portal sites**. Now, with database researching available through vendors on the Web, and banner ads offering search boxes, it is no wonder it's hard to know just what you are searching!

their sites. Now AltaVista, Lycos, Excite, and HotBot all include subject directories on their sites. So do Netscape and Microsoft.

The search engine/subject directory hybrid is now so common that there is a term for it: a portal site. Portal sites all share a common goal: to be the site that users start at every time they open up their Web browser. Portal sites all provide news coverage, stock quotes, sports scores, and some way to personalize the information presented. The "personalizing" aspects are not currently very sophisticated. You can choose whether to have TV listings or sports scores displayed, and you can choose the type of news coverage you are most interested in, but you can't set up a portal site to show you, for instance, every news article that mentions libraries.

Another hybrid that has developed is the search engine that searches a combination of freely available material from Web sites and proprietary material from periodical collections. The for-fee material can be obtained for the charge of a few dollars to your credit card—this is the "pay by the drink" strategy. Or you can purchase an individual subscription to the database, which will allow you greater access, typically a specified number of articles per month. Two organizations currently offering such hybrids are Electric Library (*www.elibrary.com*) and Northern Light (*www.northernlight.com*). Northern Light, like Yahoo, publicizes the presence of librarians on staff.

Laura Hudson, a reference librarian at Ohio University who instructs incoming freshmen about the library technology environment, notes that many people are confused by yet another recent development in the searching world: the Web-based interface to a database of information (such as popular magazine articles or abstracts of dissertations), that did not originate on the Web. Many libraries purchase institutional subscriptions to several databases of this type. But since the database interfaces look not unlike the interface on a search engine or subject directory, it's difficult for searchers to understand that they are not actually searching the Web when they search one of these Web-based databases.

Distinctions between Web search tools became even blurrier when programmers at Netscape and Internet Explorer (IE) realized that many users were simply typing their keywords directly into the Location/Address box. Programmers developed a feature that produces results from doing just that. If you type a question mark, a space, and then a few keywords into the Location/Address box in the 4.x versions of both Netscape and IE, you will be directed to a page of results from whatever search engine the browser currently has as a corporate partner.

Advertisers got into the act early as well. Many search engines display banner ads based on the keywords you type into the search box. For instance, if you search for **Divine Secrets of the Ya-Ya Sisterhood**, you will see ads appear for Amazon.com, the famous Web-based bookstore.

Perhaps the most annoying type of banner ad is one that itself incorporates a search box, which says something like "Try your search again," and has your keywords already typed into the box. When you click the button to try again, you are actually leaving the search engine's page and searching the database of an online store. This can be incredibly confusing even for the seasoned searcher.

No section on search tools would be complete without mention of the relatively recent development of filtered search engines: engines whose results are filtered for "offensive" content by one of the Internet filtering companies. These engines are just beginning to grow in popularity, but I would not be surprised if in the near future all the major engines also incorporated a "kid-safe" variant.

HOW DO YOU KEEP TRACK OF ALL THIS?

How do you keep track of all this? You don't. Most librarians have just one or two favorite Web search tools, plus a few others that they use as backup when their favorites aren't available or do not produce good results. The Web searching market is incredibly volatile. Companies will keep trying to find the ultimate bells and whistles that will bring all the searchers to them, and thus, they will keep changing their interfaces and features every few months (or weeks, in some cases). I haven't even attempted to go into the features of all the major engines (such as whether or not they permit Boolean or proximity searching or, what character they use for a wild card), because any such section would be outdated by the time this book saw print.

Fortunately, there is a site that will help you to keep track of developments in the search engine/subject directory/meta-engine/portal site world: the aptly named Search Engine Watch.

Search Engine Watch (*www.searchenginewatch.com*) is maintained by Danny Sullivan, an Internet consultant and columnist with Mecklermedia (Figure 2–1). Its purpose is to provide in-depth coverage about search engines, from tips on how to search particular engines effectively to information about which companies accept payment for top placement in their results lists. It's an extremely useful site, and you can sign up to receive Search Engine Report Newsletter, a free monthly. (You can also subscribe to the site for a fee and get access to all the back issues of the report.)

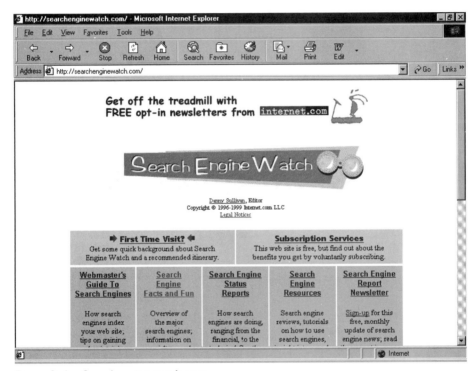

Figure 2–1   Searchenginewatch.com

MORE TOOLS

Whatis.com

The Whatis.com site (*www.whatis.com*) is extremely useful for questions relating to computers in general and the Internet environment in particular (Figures 2–2 and 2–3). The idea behind the site is simple, the creators' initial idea was to give themselves and everyone else a single place to hold everything they could find out about the Internet and computers....about "cyber-land." This is also one of the only sites I have seen that makes good use of frames-based navigation.

You can use the site in several ways. If you want to look up a specific term, you can use the alphabet across the top frame to jump to the letter you want, then click on the word you want, and the definition will appear in the bottom frame. The definitions almost always include useful links that complement the information provided. Other features of the site include a tour of How the Internet Works, which explains the Internet's infrastructure, who runs it, and where to go, and a table called The Speed of...., which explains the speeds of various carrier technologies (such as phone service, ISDN, satellite, T-1), the physical medium that enables the connection, and the application for that particular technology (home use or business use, for example). They welcome contributions of new words and ideas for more features to add.

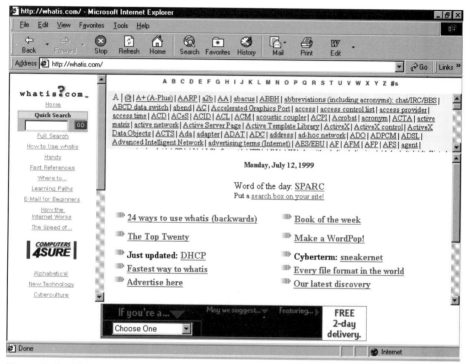

Figure 2–2   Whatis.com Opening Page

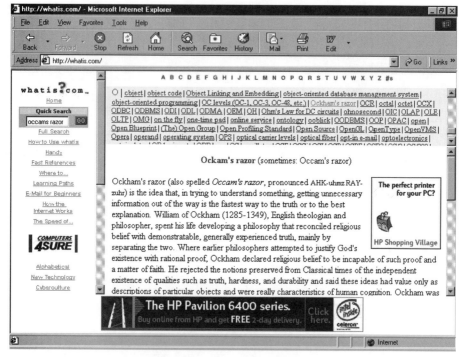

Figure 2–3   Entry for "Ockham's Razor" in Whatis.com

Ask A+ Locator

The Ask A+ Locator (*www.vrd.org/locator/*) is a feature of the Virtual Reference Desk, which itself is a project of the ERIC Clearinghouse on Information and Technology and the National Library of Education, at Syracuse University (Figures 2–4 and 2–5). The service describes itself as follows:

> The Ask A+ Locator is a database of high-quality "AskA" services designed to link students, teachers, parents, and other K–12 community members with experts on the Internet. Profiles of each AskA service include identification information (e.g., publisher, e-mail address, contact person, links to services' home pages), scope, target audience, and a general description of the service. Some of the Web sites linked from Ask A+ service profiles provide additional resources such as online reference, archives of previously asked questions, and links to related sites.

The site is particularly useful, as the description suggests, for K–12 educational topics. Teachers are frequently eager to put their students in direct contact with experts, and this database is a one-stop source for finding experts in a large number of fields.

Figure 2–4   Ask A+ Locator Opening Page

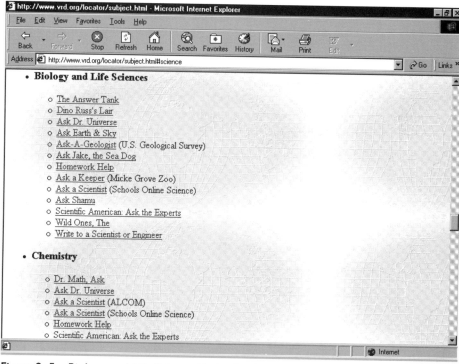

Figure 2–5   Biology and Life Science Listing for Ask A+ Locator

TWO TOOLS FOR SEARCHING NON-WEB-BASED INTERNET CONTENT

Deja.com

Though Deja (*www.deja.com*) has become substantially more commercially oriented than it was in its days as dejanews.com, it is still possible to use this tool to search the Usenet hierarchy of discussion groups (Figures 2–6 and 2–7). Go to the "Power Search" option at *www.deja.com/home_ps.shtml*, and under "Results Type," choose Deja Classic. At this writing, Deja is still providing access to Usenet posts from March 1995 to the present.

Usenet news postings can be quite useful. On particular newsgroups, subject experts maintain a presence, and they may be available to answer questions about their area of expertise. They also may have already answered a number of common questions in a FAQ (frequently asked questions) file.

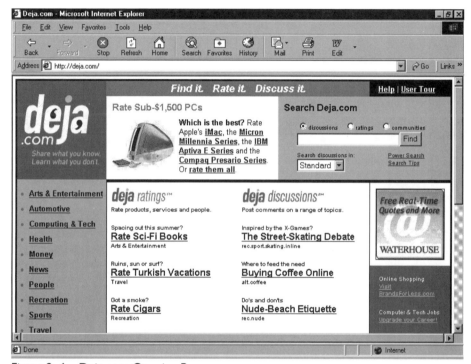

Figure 2–6   Deja.com Opening Page

Figure 2–7   Deja.com Search for **Comics**

Liszt

Liszt (*www.liszt.com*) is a service that keeps track of e-mail discussion lists (Figures 2–8 and 2–9). These lists, like Usenet, treat a vast number of topics. Lists are often hosted by academic institutions, though anyone with access to a list management software program can set up a discussion list. When you type keywords into the search box on Liszt's front page, you are searching a database of discussion groups. The entry for a particular group always includes the address of the list and instructions for subscribing. It may also include a link to a Web site maintained by the list owner, the location of the list's archives, and a description of the topics of discussion appropriate for that particular list.

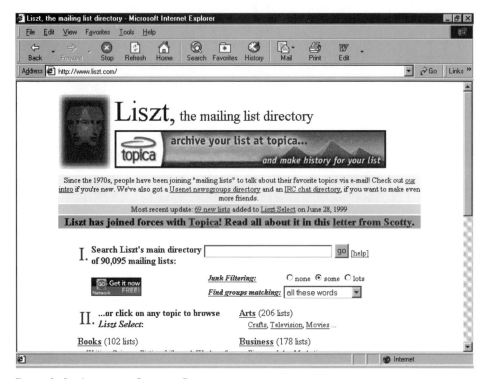

Figure 2–8   Liszt.com Opening Page

Figure 2–9   Liszt.com Search for **Comics**

WANT MORE E-MAIL?

Another good way to keep track of what's going on in the Web world is to participate in a discussion list like those mentioned previously. An astonishing number of such lists are intended for librarians. Nearly every imaginable style of librarianship is treated on one list or another. And there's even a site that keeps track of them for you: *www.wrlc.org/liblists/ /liblists.htm*. Click on the name of a list and you see instructions for subscribing and a brief description of the list's focus.

If your job includes management of Web pages or sites in addition to using the Web in a reference capacity, you should consider joining Web4Lib, a list is maintained by Roy Tennant of the University of California at Berkeley. It is "an electronic discussion for library-based World Wide Web managers." Technical questions are posted frequently, but there are also discussions about Internet-related policy issues, job postings, and announcements about new sites of interest and upcoming conferences. The archives of the list are searchable at *http:// sunsite.berkeley.edu/Web4Lib/archive.html*.

> Cybrarians' online discussion groups include Web4Lib, with its searchable archives. Many other lists for librarians are compiled at *www.wrlc.org/ liblists//liblists.htm*.

Perhaps the most important thing to remember about searching for information on the Web, whatever combination of tools you choose, is that there are people behind every site. And these people's motives for putting sites together run the gamut from altruistic to scholarly to egotistical to commercial to—sadly—evil. Information on the Web also reflects, and is tailored to, the economic level of the majority of Web users, as the increasing amount of e-commerce demonstrates. The Web forces us as librarians and as citizens to think ever more critically about where information originates, and about the biases that are present no matter what the source. (See Chapter Ten for resources that address evaluating Web site information.)

Chapter Three

Metadata: What's It to You?

Robert DeCandido

Effective searching on the Internet requires (among other things) the ability to find what you are looking for and the ability to use what you find. This chapter discusses one approach to improving the ability to discover resources—metadata—and one method of making text universally and persistently usable—SGML.

METADATA: WHAT IT IS AND WHY WE NEED IT

Anyone who has used any of the search engines available on the World Wide Web knows that it is very difficult to find exactly what you want. Searching the Internet and, in particular, that subset of it known as the World Wide Web, is notoriously difficult. Too often you are reduced to doing a search that returns too many hits, often tens of thousands, and then wading through that information to find what you really wanted. The crucial reason for this is that, though the Internet is rife with data, it is very poor in metadata. Metadata is a new name for a very old concept. It is sometimes explained as information about information. Though some disparage this definition (and, indeed it is somewhat tautological) it nonetheless conveys the idea that metadata describes and defines a body of information. Even more important it suggests that metadata is a succinct body of information about a larger body of information. As such it provides an efficient way to find the information it references. (The classic example of the power of metadata is that endangered species beloved of some reactionary scholars, the card catalog. If the cards only consisted of a freeform synopsis of each book, it would still be quicker to search through a drawer of cards than read through hundreds of books. If the author, title, or subject have been identified and alphabetized, the power and speed of this information retrieval system has been vastly enhanced.) So let us modify our definition of metadata to say that it is *a succinct and systematic set of information that references, and can be used to retrieve efficiently and accurately, a larger set of information.*

Consider now the World Wide Web. Pull up a Web page and see what metadata is present or even deducible. There may be something tagged as a title if you look at the HTML code, but it may be no more helpful than Home. The title may appear as a header on the page or it may be buried in an image file that you can read on the screen but that a computer does not recognize as words. There is, in short, little or no metadata that any system can identify that will allow it to retrieve that title with any great degree of certainty that it is making an appropriate choice. Given this shortcoming most search engines must fall back on other, less accurate ways of determining relevancy, such as word frequency and placement near the beginning of a document. Clearly any degree of consistent metadata would give query engines something better to work with. Unfortunately the most readily available metadata system for information retrieval, AACR2 and the MARC record standard used by libraries, is far too unwieldy to be used on Web resources—it would be like cataloging each page of every book. Something less elaborate is needed.

THE DUBLIN CORE

Several groups are working on simpler, more manageable metadata schemes for the Web. A good place to learn about some of that metadata activity is *www.w3.org/Metadata/*. One initiative, the Platform for Internet Content Selection, or PICS, is concerned mostly with issues of rating, filtering, and privacy.

Of greater interest here is the Dublin Core set of metadata elements, designed to aid automated discovery and retrieval of information on the Internet. It is an attempt to codify a small and simple set of information that can be used to describe any Internet resource. Though it is still developing, it is likely that ten basic elements will form a core metadata set. This seems to be a manageable amount of information particularly since all of the elements are conceived of as optional. They are: name, identifier, version, registration authority, language, definition, obligation, datatype, maximum occurrence, and comment.

(For a description of what these elements are meant to include see *http://purl.org/dc/elements/1.1.*) This element set can be used to build a catalog or database or be encoded directly into the HTML (or SGML or XML) used to create Web documents. Direct encoding is likely to be the way the Dublin Core will most often be used. Metadata can be coded into the head of a Web document, which is reserved for information that is not intended to display in the browser.

Following (page 40) is a sample of Dublin Core and other metadata from the home page of the Visual Arts Data Service (*http://vads.ahds.ac.uk/*) in England. The Dublin Core elements include DC as part of the element name (for example, META NAME="DC. Description.")

```
<HEAD>
<TITLE>Visual Arts Data Service home page</TITLE>
<META NAME="description" CONTENT="Visual Arts Data
  Service">
<META NAME="DC.Description" CONTENT="(LANG = en)
  The home page for the Visual Arts Data Ser-
  vice, A JISC funded service to provide networked
  digital resources for the  UK higher education
  community in the visual arts. VADS also advises
  on standards of good practice for the creation,
  description and preservation of digital infor-
  mation">
<META NAME="keywords" CONTENT="visual arts data
  service, vads, arts & humanities data service,
  ahds, preservation">
<META NAME="DC.Title" CONTENT="Visual Arts Data
  Service">
<META NAME="DC.Subject" CONTENT="visual arts data
  service, vads, arts & humanities data service,
  ahds, preservation">
<META NAME="DC.Author"  CONTENT="(TYPE=homepage)
  http://vads.ahds.ac.uk/">
<META NAME="DC.Date.Created" CONTENT="(SCHEME = ISO
  31-1) 1996-12-10">
<META NAME="DC.Date.LastModified" CONTENT="(SCHEME
  = ISO 31-1) 1998-01-08">
<META NAME="DC.Format" CONTENT="(SCHEME=imt) text/
  html">
<META NAME="DC.Identifier"  CONTENT="(TYPE=url)
  http://vads.ahds.ac.uk/">
<META NAME="DC.Relation.IsChildOf" CONTENT="(TYPE
  =childof) http://ahds.ac.uk">
<META NAME="DC.Rights" CONTENT="http://vads.ahds.ac.
  uk/Rights.html">
<META NAME="DC.Language"  CONTENT="(SCHEME=iso639)
  en">
<META NAME="GENERATOR" CONTENT="Mozilla/3.03Gold
  (Win95; I) [Netscape]">
</HEAD>
```

HOW IT WILL BE USED

Currently none of the major search engines know how to read Dublin Core metadata. The developers are hoping that enough scholarly projects will use the element set to demonstrate its utility (*www.oclc.org/oclc/research/projects/core/projects/index.htm*). In the meantime other types of descriptive metadata are being developed. Communities do not find the MARC data structure with its orientation toward books and publications very useful, but people who work in the visual arts and geospatial studies are also developing metadata schemes that meet their particular needs. A major concern of the metadata community (and such a community is emerging) is the need to map information between metadata schemes. There is already a method for transferring information between MARC and Dublin Core, and other such maps are being developed. The Dublin Core could thus act as a sort of base element set for a first level of searching that could either find data or lead to more specific and complex metadata.

Whether this mapping happens depends on programmers developing and searchers using tools that recognize the structured data created utilizing the Dublin Core or other metadata schemes. When and if that occurs, searching the Internet will become a much more sophisticated, efficient, and satisfying process.

Spamdexing

The <META> tags used by the Dublin Core can also be used to enter unstructured keywords. With little else to grab onto, search engines can use these keywords to retrieve information. Like so much else on the Internet this capability is susceptible to abuse. Popular search terms can be entered as keywords by the creator regardless of their relevancy to the rest of the document. This practice can significantly increase the number of hits on a page and allow the owner to increase advertising rates or just enjoy the adolescent pleasure of having fooled a lot of people. Search engines try to ignore or at least reduce the relevancy rating of these false hits, but some will get through anyway. If you find a completely irrelevant page in the middle of a search result you're probably the victim of spamdexing.

SGML: WHAT IT IS AND WHY WE NEED IT

By now we have all had the problem of trying to read and use computer files created by programs that have been superseded. Perhaps you have documents that you created with WordStar back in the ancient days or a spreadsheet you made using Framework. Can your new, spiffy Windows program read them? Or, perhaps, you've switched from Mac to PC or vice versa. Which of your old files will you be able to read? Consider how much greater is the problem for a company whose entire document inventory (manuals, parts lists, technical papers, and the like) has been made with one program or another that encodes the files with its own particular and proprietary coding. Consider, too, a library that wishes to make available online the text of some of its collections. Neither of these organizations can afford to be caught in the position of throwing away or redoing work already done and paid for. Neither wishes to be dependent on software manufacturers and programmers to keep their data usable. The only way to escape this difficulty is to develop a public standard using universally accepted and standardized codes that all operating systems and programs could read and employ. This is exactly what *Standard Generalized Markup Language (SGML) is.*

SGML employs *ASCII (American Standard Code for Information Interchange)* to represent text. It is, simply, a standard that assigns numeric equivalents (all that a computer understands) for all characters (such as letters, numbers, or punctuation marks) that can be input into a computer through a keyboard. So, for instance, the quantity 71 is the equivalent of *G*, 103 equals *g*, 64 is the @ symbol, and so on. Virtually all computer systems understand this code. This one standard underlies the two most successful aspects of the Internet: e-mail (which is based on the interchange of ASCII code); and the World Wide Web (which uses a form of SGML known as *HTML*, or *Hypertext Markup Language*).

Anyone who has seen or worked with HTML has a good idea of how SGML works. The text of a document is annotated or marked up with information about it. These annotations are also text but enclosed in special characters to distinguish them from the rest of the text. So, for instance, you might have text that reads:

<P>He told him <I>not</I> to play with the knife.</P>

If the computer reading this text knows that this is part of an HTML document, it will know that <P> is a mark or tag that means the beginning of a paragraph and that </P> means the end of a paragraph. It will also know when the italics begin and end by the <I> and </I> tags. It will know these things because they are laid out in a Document Type Definition (DTD), which defines HTML and states what may be used as tags and where and how those tags may be used. SGML allows the user to create DTDs for any kind of document. In fact it is, basically, a set of rules for creating DTDs. HTML is mostly concerned with how a document displays on a computer screen—such as how large the type is, whether it is centered, whether it is bold. Yet HTML, which is all well and good and extraordinarily popular, only scratches the surface of what might be done by marking up text.

SGML can be used in a number of ways: names, titles, and subjects can all be identified and searched as such; text can be analyzed and structured; indexes can be developed; links between texts (and between texts and other digital data such as images and databases) can be constructed. SGML is so flexible that a DTD can be developed to accommodate almost any use. Given the proper tagging (and the time, people, and money to do it) there is almost no limit to the amount of information and intelligence that can be added to text, thus leading the structural advantages of a database without losing the discursive advantages of text. For these reasons SGML has found widespread use in the government, military, and commerce. Academia has also found a home for SGML in the digitizing of literary and historical texts. For an idea of how diverse the use of SGML is, see Cover, Robin, SGML/XML Applications: Government, Military, and Heavy Industry; (*www.oasis-open.org/cover/gov-apps.html*) and Cover, Robin, SGML/XML Academic Applications (*www.oasis-open.org/cover/acadapps.html*).

Meta Acronyms

SGML = Standard Generalized Markup Language, a scheme using codes that all operating systems and programs could read and employ.

HTML = Hyptertext Markup Language, a form of SGML used on the World Wide Web.

DTD = Document Type Definition, defines HTML and states what may be used as tags and how tags may be used.

XML = Extensible Markup Language, modifies SGML structure without the limitations of HTML or the difficulties of SGML.

TEI = Text Encoding Initiative, a DTD.

EAD = Encoding Archival Description, a DTD.

With all these advantages, why, one must wonder, has SGML not become the standard for everything on the Internet and off. One reason is that it is relatively new. SGML only became a standard in 1986. Another is that there are short-term advantages to software manufacturers if their programs create files in proprietary code. Such code encourages, even enforces, a sort of user loyalty, and it gives the manufacturer control of product development.

Finally and perhaps most important, SGML is so large and so flexible it is difficult to create applications that create or use it. The popularity of the World Wide Web is based largely on the simplicity of HTML. Authors have only one standard to learn. Developers can create browsers for this one simple DTD and build applications that interact with it because it is (variants notwithstanding) a single set of elements and a single standard way of encoding them. To take full advantage of SGML, authors would have to know how to create DTDs, and browsers would have to be able to read any file created with any DTD. Browsers would also have to know how to display each kind of file. (HTML gets around this problem by making display an implicit part of its DTD.) Currently SGML can only be read by specialized browsers. If a library or university wishes to make its SGML files available to the public, it must either implement a program on its server to translate the SGML into HTML or it must rely on its users to have or get a browser that can read SGML directly.

These quite significant difficulties are being addressed by the creation of *Extensible Markup Language (XML)*. By modifying the basic SGML structure and rules to make them less flexible (and less elegant), XML's creators hope to create a language that will retain the power of SGML without the limitations of HTML or the difficulties of SGML. Documents created using XML may or may not have a DTD—browsers should be able to read them without one. The progress of XML looks promising when a recent article (May 1999) in *Scientific American* touts it. (See also the Public Library Association's Tech Note on Metadata, (*http://www.pla.org/metadata.htm*). When and whether all these claims are made good will determine the future of the Internet. It will also determine the stability and accessibility of the information residing there.

USING AND SEARCHING SGML RESOURCES

One of the major uses for SGML has been for the production of internal, private documents in commerce and in the military. There are, though, two forms of SGML, two DTDs, that are being used to create publicly accessible documents. These are Text Encoding Initiative (TEI) files, which are used primarily for transcribing literary texts and primary source material, and Encoded Archival Description (EAD). The number of these files available on the Web is growing daily and they are beginning to offer significant resources for researchers. They are different enough from other Web resources to warrant a brief discussion of their peculiarities.

Finding Aids Online

Over the centuries archivists have developed methods of describing the contents and organization of archival collections. Recently those methods have become more standardized. In 1993, building on this new consensus, the University of California at Berkeley began developing a standard for encoding archive and library finding aids in the form of an SGML DTD. The final result of this project is Version 1.0 of the EAD Document Type Definition, which was made public at the end of 1998. (A description of this project is available at *http://sunsite.berkeley.edu/ FindingAids/findaids.html.*)

Even before Version 1.0 was adopted a number of institutions began using the beta version to create and recreate their archival finding aids. There are at least two reasons for this enthusiasm. EAD finding aids are very effective Web documents: because they are highly regularized and customized they provide researchers with better tools for seeing and navigating the complex organizational structures that archives often require. Even more important, the EAD forces consistency between finding aids in the same institution and even between institutions. This means that researchers can be given the opportunity to search many finding aids at once regardless of their location. These benefits are evident in two exemplary multi-institution projects—the Dance Heritage Coalition's Dance Research Resources: Finding Aids for Archival Collections (*http:/ /digilib.nypl.org/dynaWeb/dhc/findaid/@Generic__CollectionView*); and UC Berkeley's American Heritage Virtual Archive Project (*http:// sunsite.berkeley.edu/amher/*).

An aspect of the EAD that has so far been largely unexploited is the ability to link digital images directly to the finding aid. In other words: a finding aid citation is linked directlly to an image of the document, picture, or other item cited. When this is done, the finding aid becomes not just a description of an archive but a representation of it that will be available worldwide to anyone with Web access.

Electronic Texts

For many years we have heard that all the libraries in the world will soon be available online. That dream has been going around since computers were invented, and one could not help but be amused by how blithely the people who said such things took the enormity of that task. Even today with the stunning growth of the Internet it seems unlikely that we will ever put together the time, money, and resources to convert our entire documentary patrimony. Nonetheless, some of that heritage is worth the expense to convert—indeed some of it already has been converted and much more will follow soon. Only a year after SGML was formulated in 1986, a planning conference was convened by the Association for Computers and the Humanities to begin creating what was to become the Text Encoding Initiative (TEI) DTD. (A brief history of the development of this standard can be read at *www-tei.uic.edu/orgs/ tei/info/hist.html.*)

The TEI DTD is so large and complex that it can and has been used for a multitude of transcriptional applications, from (transliterated) Japanese texts to the works of African-American women writers to Chaucer. A list of applications using TEI is available at *www-tei.uic.edu/orgs/tei/ app/index.html.*

Searching SGML

As all searchers know, the AND Boolean operator is not very useful in full-text searches; proximity and adjacency searches are more effective. This fact is particularly true in searching SGML resources. Were you to search the text of a novel for **dog AND food** the result would only tell you whether both those words appeared anywhere in the text. A search specifying that the word *dog* be within 3 words of *food* would give results likely to relate to feeding canines. There are a number of ways this sort of search may be implemented and a good SGML resource should guide users in its application. One example may be seen at NYPL's Digital Schomburg African-American Women Writers of the 19th Century (*http://digital.nypl.org/schomburg/writers_aa19/*) (Figure 3–1).

Because SGML tags identify delimited segments of text, an SGML document can be treated as a database with different fields. For instance it is possible to search a group of texts for terms that appear only in chapter headings or only in title pages. What is available to the researcher will depend on exactly how and how extensively a text has been tagged. Some historical manuscripts have been so closely analyzed and encoded that you can search for the text created by a particular scribe or search for terms. Most researchers are not expert in SGML, and they will need

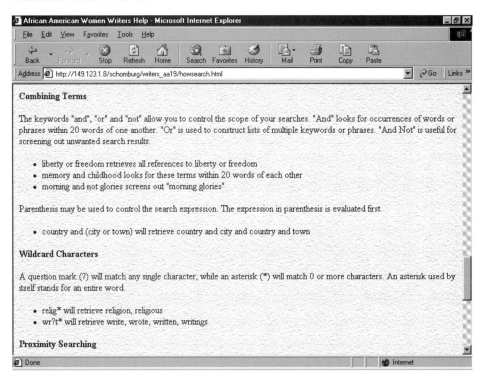

Figure 3–1 NYPS's Digital Schomburg African-American Women Writers of the 19th Century

guidance to use this capability. The University of Virginia Modern English Collection of electronic texts (*http://etext.virginia.edu/etcbin/ ot2www-eng2?specfile=/lv4/modeng/www/modeng-pub.o2w*) is a good example of using Web-based forms to assist users in exploiting the strengths of SGML tagging (Figure 3–2).

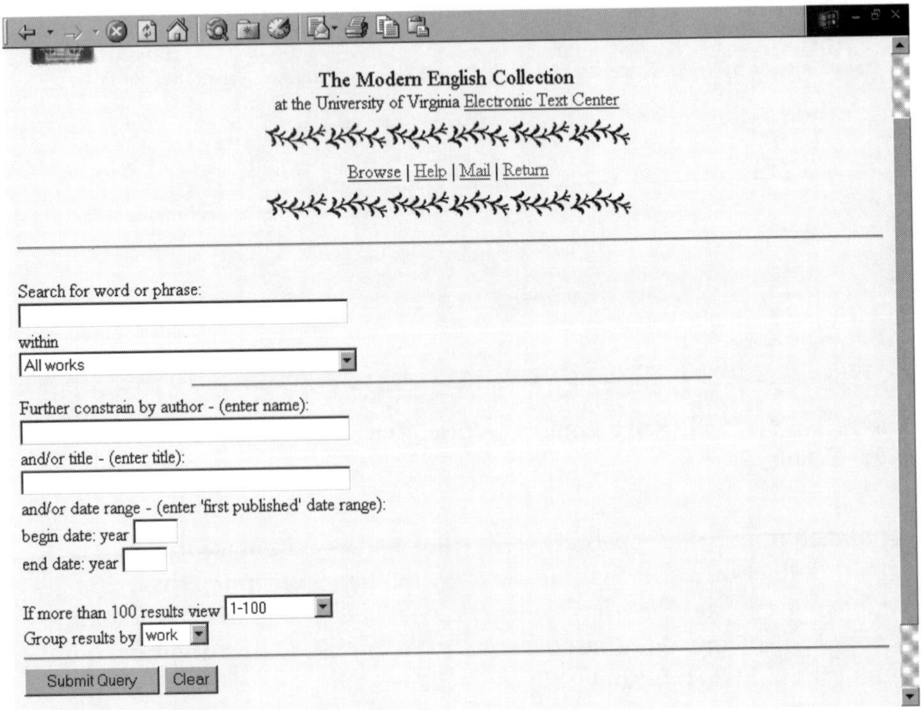

The Modern English Collection
at the University of Virginia Electronic Text Center

Browse | Help | Mail | Return

Search for word or phrase:

within

All works

Further constrain by author - (enter name):

and/or title - (enter title):

and/or date range - (enter 'first published' date range):

begin date: year

end date: year

If more than 100 results view 1-100

Group results by work

Submit Query   Clear

Figure 3–2 Web Forms in the University of Virginia's Modern English Collection of Electronic Texts

IN THE SWEET BY-AND-BY

If the contents of the world's libraries (or even any significant portion of them) are ever to be "put on computer," it is most likely to be in the form of SGML or a close descendant of it. Creating, serving out, searching, and using SGML will become an essential part of every library. Understanding and exploiting it will be an important part of every librarian's and researcher's skills.

Chapter Four

Bots and Intelligent Agents

Steve Ruddy

At MIT during the 1960s the computer research scientists were spending much of their time carefully backing up their files every day. This was a tiresome but necessary process. Professor Fernando Corbato decided to create software to automate this routine, and one of the first bots was born.

Bot, as you probably suspect, comes from the word *robot*. The word is derived from *robata*, which means "work" in Czech. Bots come in a variety of flavors. There are "spiders," bots that traverse the Web gathering information on Web sites; "newsbots," which will keep their eye on news sites and even Usenet newsgroups for predefined subjects and keywords; "chatterbots" that speak to you and, depending on how cleverly they are designed, may have not revealed themselves to be an artificial lifeform; "linkbots" that will scan a specified URL and report back to you on the status of your hyperlinks and other factors.

Many other types of bots are out there roaming the World Wide Web as you read this, and they are not necessarily good-natured. One example is a "spambot," which is as distasteful as it sounds. However, most bots exist to make the Web easier for the user to navigate and to understand.

There is also a species of bot known as an "intelligent agent." An intelligent agent promises to do more than merely automate tedious tasks

> The word *bot* comes from *robot*, a word invented in the 1920 play *R.U.R.* by Czech writer Karel Capek. R.U.R. stands for Rossum's Universal Robots.

for the end user. An *agent* is commonly defined as something that acts on behalf of something else. The use of the word *intelligent* has been a bit more difficult to define. In the early days of artificial intelligence, *intelligence* meant true replication of human cognizance by a machine. Many scientists struggled to make this replication possible, but none have succeeded. However there were successes in creating bots, which seemed to have a sophisticated level of intelligence because they had sophisticated search, retrieval, and decision-making programming. This is the nature of the word *intelligence* used in the term today—the machine rather than human intelligence. Researchers also discovered that they were more likely to succeed if they did not try to replicate the human mind, but rather to create agent software that was useful to humans.

You have probably used a bot to help you wade through the large amounts of information on the Web in the past, perhaps without even knowing it. Many popular search engines use bots to gather information about the Web. They travel the World Wide Web day and night collecting the Web site information used to create the searchable indexes we all know and love. Search engines maintained by bots include Infoseek, AltaVista, and HotBot. These bots were originally intended to search through metadata on Web pages in order to create relevant hits. However, people took advantage of this process and what is commonly known as spamdexing was born (see the box on spamdexing in Chapter Three). People fooled search engine rankings by listing their keywords over and over again, so that sites with such repetitions appeared to the bot to be the most relevant hits. Some abusers were also inclined to list very popular search terms even if they were not relevant to their particular sites. This in turn caused the search engines to change their strategies and ignore metatags.

Please note that not all search engines are automated through the use of robots; some rely on the human indexers. There are also myriad specialized Web search bots, which usually focus on a particular subject: the Botspot likes Ferret, Alexa, and BullsEye, for example.

SHOPBOTS

Another bot attracting attention these days is the shopbot. With the promise of widespread secure e-commerce on the Web, you will be able to purchase from a much larger selection of retailers. With the many Internet shopping sites online today and the millions more to come in the near future, how could you ever take advantage of having so much

Figure 4–1 Excite Product Finder (powered by Jango)

to choose from? Enter the shopbot, a digital assistant that searches the Web and reports the prices offered by Internet retailers for a particular item you need. Take all this a step further and have your shopbot go out and negotiate with other shopbots for a lowest price, bartering and haggling. There are a number of shopbots in existence, and I'm sure more on the way. On the Excite site (Figure 4–1), you can find shopping services powered by the shopbot Jango (*http://jango.excite.com/xsh/ index.dcg?*). The Jango interface is easy to use and returns results quickly. You have the choice of searching through the Auction or Classified sites with this bot. To use, first select a product category from the menu. I chose Furbys from the Games and Toys column. You can enter additional descriptive information if necessary and select the Find Prices button. Within 30 seconds I had leads and prices for obtaining a Furby from eight different sources. Not bad compared to waiting for the local toy store to open and then battling hundreds of other people for a chance to own one.

NEWSBOTS

A newsbot is an agent that searches the Web and retrieves news stories based on user-defined criteria. One example is Knight Ridder's Newshound (*www.newshound.com*). Newshound searches the full-content of the *San José Mercury News* as well as a number of other full content news sources. There are three steps to working with Newshound. First, you must train your hound. Training involves determining what type of information you are looking for. Second, you choose your delivery method. The method of delivery can be in the form of e-mail or HTML delivered to the Newshound site. You can have the site e-mail you each story as it is found or send the whole thing as a digest scheduled at your convenience. The third step is viewing the results.

LINK CHECKERS

A common practice of many Internet searchers is to compile a Web page of listing links they consider to be useful. We have all used such pages as a starting point for research. We have all probably noticed also that, due to the chaotic nature of the Web, many of these links break very quickly (commonly called link-rot) and we get error messages instead of the useful information we were expecting. Maintaining these types of pages quickly becomes a large task.

There are bots, known as link checkers, to assist us in such endeavors; one of the most popular is Linkbot (*www.tetranetsoftware.com/products/linkbot.htm*) by Tetranet Software. Linkbot allows you to specify the starting point of your link checking, how many levels you want to follow down, and whether you want it to go off site; you can also adjust as necessary many other user-determined options for creating a Linkbot report. When you are ready, you run the program, which begins searching through the specified territory for broken links. When it is finished, Linkbot creates an HTML report alerting you to everything that needs attending on the specified pages. This report can speed up your site maintenance, help inspire user confidence, and prevent the headaches that often occur when you show someone your site and error messages start popping up. There is a free version of Linkbot called Linkbot Express available on the Tetranet site.

BOT EXCLUSION

With all of these robots running around the Web, poking around in your files, you might be wondering if some bots could possibly cause harm to your files or server. The truth of the matter is yes, there is always that possibility. It is due more to poorly designed robots than software created with a malicious intent. For example a bot that crawls a server and hits your links in a rapid-fire manner has the potential to create a burden on your server, bringing it to a crashing halt. You may wonder whether you want to take such chances. This is where the Robot Exclusion Standard (*http://info.webcrawler.com/mak/projects/robots/norobots.html#status*) comes into play. This standard allows you to specify rules for robots attempting to access your site. You may wish to allow only certain bots the right to traverse your data and this can be done by setting up a robots.txt file on your server. This file will also allow you to specify certain areas of your server as off limits to robots. The details of the robots.txt file can be found on the Web Robots pages.

Another method of preventing bots from running amok through your files is in the form of an HTML <META> tag. This tag allows you to specify whether robots can index your site and whether you wish them to follow your links. An example of a statement that allows your site to be accessed by all robots would look like this and appear in the head of your document:

<META NAME="ROBOTS" CONTENT="ALL">

You can find out more about exclusion in Dr. Clue's HTML guide (*www.drclue.net*). Note that not all robots are responsive to this method of exclusion.

AGENTS

Microsoft has developed MSAgent (*www.microsoft.com/workshop/imedia/agent/agentdl.asp*), which it provides free to users. This is an interesting collection of software with an even more interesting possible future. You can download the agent application, a text-to-speech synthesizer, a character editor, and even a voice recognition engine from their site. These agents are three-dimensional puppets, which can move around the screen, talk to you, and much more. This is a good place to start for those interested in creating their own Web agents, as the technology is available free, is well documented, has a wide base of fan support, and offers a few third-party applications that will help you create scripts for using agents on your Web pages. The downside is that MSAgent only works in Internet Explorer 4.x on machines that have downloaded the agent application. Watching MSAgent demos makes one feel that we are much closer to the digital librarians of the Cyberpunk movement than we thought. There is an online banking demo on the Argolink site (*www.argolink.com*), for example, which takes the user through an imaginary bank transaction and requires MSAgent. Other agent applications are tied into map generation systems, chat networks, and even the Windows Explorer. For the most part, Microsoft agents currently serve as site guides, providing use instruction and answering questions about products offered by the site owners.

IBM is also betting on the future of agent technology. Their goal is to develop intelligent agent technology that is easy to integrate with a broad range of networked applications. Although IBM is no longer distributing Agent Building Environment (ABE) developer's toolkit, as of 1997, the former Intelligent Agents Project at IBM T.J. Watson Research (1994–1997) has grown and transmuted into what IBM calls "several different agents-y projects." (*www.research.ibm.com/jargents/ibm*)

1. *Business Rules for Electronic Commerce*: fundamental core technology and pilot applications, about intelligent rule-based agents in e-commerce. In particular, it is developing the CommonRules alpha prototype, a Java library of business rules capabilities, that supersumes almost all of the functionality of IBM Agent Building Environment (ABE). The first alpha version of CommonRules is scheduled to be released (free, with trial license) on IBM's *AlphaWorks* in late summer, 1999.
2. *Information Economies*: investigating market economies composed of multiple intelligent agents, including micro-economic interactions (and decision making) and macro-economic emergent phenomena, especially for information goods and services.
3. *MailCat*: a learning assistant for categorizing e-mail—essentially, an intelligent agent.

More information about bots is available at the Botspot (*www.botspot.com*). The Botspot features a Bot of the Week with complete archives of past Bots of the Week. Another great site for bot information is Links 2 Go (*www.links2go.com/topic/Agents*). It serves as a jumping-off point to many other agent technology sites. You can also find many other sites of this type using conventional search techniques. This overview is only a sampling of what is available to the Internet searcher today. Hundreds

---

BOT Links

Shopbots
Jango-*jango.excite.com/xsh/index.dcg?*

Newsbots
Newshound-*www.newshound.com/*

Link checkers
Linkbot *www.tetranetsoftware.com/products/linkbot.htm*

Robot Exclusion Standards
Robot Exclusion Standards *info.webcrawler.com/mak/projects/robots/norobots.html#status*

Robots
www.drclue.net/

Microsoft Agent links
Microsoft
www.microsoft.com/workshop/imedia/agent/agentdl.asp

Argolink (Internet Genie Bank)
www.argolink.com/

IBM CommonRules
www.research.ibm.com/iagents/ibm

General Bot sites and info
The Botspot
www.botspot.com

Links 2 Go Agent links
www.links2go.com/topic/Agents

---

of bots have been created to help you search the Web quickly and easily. Once you become familiar with bots and know which ones you want to use, you will be able to do far more with the Net.

Chapter Five

Using the Internet for Research: Building Web Guides

Peter Morville, revised by GraceAnne A. DeCandido

To conduct research is to search or investigate carefully and exhaustively. Variations on the definition range from comprehensive academic research within a particular discipline to less structured research on a personal topic of interest. A university professor searching through piles of bibliographies for academic articles about molecular engineering is conducting research. So is the hobbyist trying to compile a list of model railroad clubs, conferences, and events around the country.

Although many of the same search tools are useful in conducting ad hoc or reference queries, the goals and processes of research are very different. The goal of an ad hoc query is to find the answer to a specific question. The goal of a research investigation is to find all or most of the information on a particular topic. Reference queries are usually short and simple. Research queries tend to extend over days, weeks, or months, be highly iterative and interactive, and involve a wide range of tools and resources. Traditional research tools include library catalogs, reference books, microfilms, CD-ROMs, commercial online databases, and the telephone. Some tools are relatively new while others have been around for hundreds of years.

Some would have us believe that the global Internet is the ultimate research tool. Digital libraries, electronic journals, image databases, and hypermedia encyclopedias put information from around the world at our fingertips. Intelligent agents scour the networks searching for new information to index. Powerful search engines with well-designed query interfaces provide intellectual access to this vast ocean of knowledge.

This dream of an Internet information utopia that provides one-stop shopping for professional researchers and amateur hobbyists alike is a long way from being realized. The contents of most books, journals, magazines, technical reports, and databases are not available via the Internet. In fact, when compared with the volume of information available in print, the Internet's vast oceans seem more like lakes or puddles. Today's Internet is a distributed chaotic environment that changes every day. The most useful information resources of today may be gone tomorrow. Servers crash and phone lines go down. Resources vary tremendously with respect to quality, currency, and level of organization. There is no editorial board and no enforceable standard for content. Information on the Internet may be out of date, misleading, or just plain wrong. To make things worse, there's no top-down organizational hierarchy and no card catalog or OPAC for cyberspace. Locating useful information can be as difficult as finding a needle in a haystack.

> The goal of an ad hoc query is to find the answer to a specific question. The goal of a research investigation is to find all or most of the information on a particular topic.

Despite these problems, the Internet does provide access to a growing body of information that is far less accessible via the traditional research tools. Government publications, product and service information, technical data, software programs, and weather statistics are just some of the information resources that are most easily accessible via the Internet. The distributed and digital nature of the Internet lends itself well to information that changes constantly and must be gathered from multiple locations. Since any individual or organization can make information available, we tend to see great volumes of sales and marketing literature, political commentary, travel advertisements, and so on. The Internet is an information space to which anyone can contribute, and they do. Much of the information is useless but some can be very useful. Skilled researchers learn to make use of the various tools and resources for sifting through this ocean of data for the information they need.

The collection of tools and resources for conducting Internet research is rich and varied. Virtual libraries, Internet directories, search engines, and communities of people are all available to help in the search. Some

Government publications, product and service information, technical data, software programs, and weather statistics are just some of the information resources that are most easily accessible via the Internet. The distributed and digital nature of the Internet lends itself well to information that changes constantly and must be gathered from multiple locations.

search tools, such as Lycos and Open Text, are highly automated, employing intelligent software agents and powerful search engines. Others, such as the Argus Clearinghouse, integrate human effort and software tools to provide topical access to information resources. None of these tools provides a complete solution. To search or investigate carefully, the researcher must integrate a number of complementary tools. Internet resource discovery is an iterative and interactive process in which a searcher makes use of virtual libraries, directories, search engines, and communities of people to find Internet information resources. An Internet directory might lead to an online community where someone mentions an electronic journal that points to a virtual library, and so on. It's important to keep in mind that Internet resource discovery is more an art than a science. The Internet's chaotic and ever-changing nature will ensure that some of the tools and resources described in this book will be replaced over the coming months and years. However, the basic principles and heuristics of conducting Internet research described here should endure as the environment evolves.

THE RESEARCH PROCESS

Perhaps the best way to illustrate the iterative and interactive nature of Internet research is to lead you through a sample guide-building project from beginning to end. For the purposes of this section, imagine that Susan, a librarian at the University of Athens, has been contacted by John, a professor in her university's biology department. The professor is interested in exploring the potential for incorporating Internet resources into his environmental studies curriculum. After some discussion, Susan and John decide that a topical guide to environmental resources on the Internet might be the best way to introduce the students to the Internet. Susan will develop the guide and John will provide assistance where necessary.

Selecting a Topic

Selecting a specific topic for the guide is the first step. Because environmental studies is a very broad area, Susan and John discuss narrowing the focus to ecology, the branch of science concerned with the interrelationship of organisms and their environment. John provides Susan with some background material on the field and explains the types of information that would be most useful to his students. He also provides a list of related keywords, such as *ecosystem, biodiversity, symbiosis,* and *preservation*. Having selected the topic, Susan is ready to start the research. Susan searches the Argus Clearinghouse: she goes from Environment on its home page, to the Environment subcategory of Ecology, to its list of 37 guides on ecology (Figure 5–1).

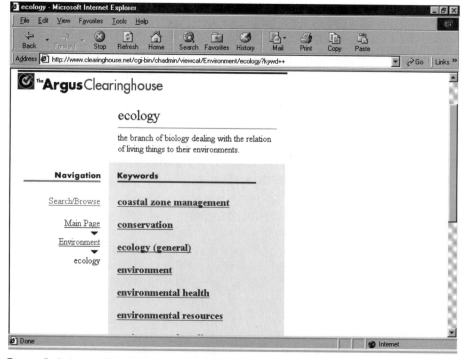

Figure 5–1 Argus Clearinghouse list for **Ecology,** *http://www.clearinghouse.net/cgi-bin/chadmin/viewcat/Environment/ecology?kywd++>*

Virtual Libraries

Virtual libraries or value-added collections of Internet resources are a great place to begin. The primary strength of virtual libraries arises from the fact that real live people (sometimes called "cybrarians") have added value to these collections through the identification, selection, description, evaluation, and organization of resources. Essentially, these cybrarians create subject-oriented guides or Web sites for use by the Internet community. Topics covered in virtual libraries are often covered in great depth; they are often preselected and well organized. On the down side, virtual libraries do not tend to be comprehensive in their coverage of topics, and the currency of resources depends on the busy schedules of the people who maintain them. Virtual libraries are typically organized by topic. Users browse through the hierarchical subject trees from level to level. Some virtual libraries provide search capabilities, but browsing is the primary means of navigation.

A good virtual library to begin with is the Argus Clearinghouse, where Susan already conducted her preliminary survey and found 37 links to further resources. Susan then moves on to visit the World Wide Web Virtual Library. Its section called Ecology, Biodiversity and the Environment is now at Rice University.

Internet Directories

Susan then decides to visit an Internet directory or collection of resources maintained by the global Internet community. With several million potential contributors, the strength of Internet directories clearly lies in their ability to be relatively comprehensive and current. The primary disadvantage lies in the lack of editorial control over content and organization. Within limits, anyone can add any information to these directories, so the quality varies widely. Coverage tends to be broad rather than deep. You can find information on almost any topic, but not a lot of information on each topic. Directories typically provide options for browsing and searching. As they grow in depth and breadth, the browsing feature becomes less useful while the searching capabilities become increasingly important. Susan begins with Yahoo, the largest and most popular of the directories. Susan selects Science from the main menu, then Ecology from the list of subcategories. There are 475 entries under that topic (in the first edition of this book, there were 50).

Search Engines for Finding Information, Software, and People

Having explored the virtual libraries and Internet directories, Susan is ready to employ some of the Internet search engines. Search engines constitute the most diverse category of Internet resources. Some permit fielded queries using Boolean logic while others provide only a simple keyword search of full-text documents. Newer search engines, such as AskJeeves, permit searching in "natural language"—the way people actually ask questions. Search engines may be used to search for information, software, people, or communities of people. The common characteristic of these tools is the provision of keyword searching capabilities in contrast to the emphasis on browsing hierarchical topic trees that we find in the virtual libraries and Internet directories. Susan begins with Lycos (Figure 5–2). She finds four matching categories (News, Politics, People, and Education); and more than 15 pages of links with all kinds of information. (In another indication of how the Web has changed since the first edition, she also sees ads for books she can purchase about ecology and for "related" music).

Susan then moves on to use some of the tools for finding communities of people. She already has a list of Usenet newsgroups and e-mail discussion groups that she found in the Argus Clearinghouse, but she'd like to search for more. Using a tool called Publicly Accessible Mailing Lists (PAML), Susan finds about two dozen e-mail discussion groups on the topic of ecology; when she checks Liszt, she finds 54. PAML and Liszt provide brief descriptions of the groups as well as information about how to subscribe and participate (Figure 5–3).

Susan then uses a tool called Deja.com to search through an immense collection of Usenet newsgroups. A search for **ecology** produces over 2,500 results, presented as a list of postings with the name of the newsgroup and the person who submitted the posting. Deja.com helps her to find some interesting groups including sci.bio.ecology (Figure 5–4) and sci.environment. Susan starts to monitor each of these groups using her Usenet news reader to get a sense of the volume and quality of the postings.

Susan has now completed the initial research phase of her guide-building process. She has browsed through virtual libraries and Internet directories, employed the keyword querying capabilities of search engines, and identified interesting online communities of people. She's now ready to turn her attention toward the development of her guide to ecology-related resources on the Internet.

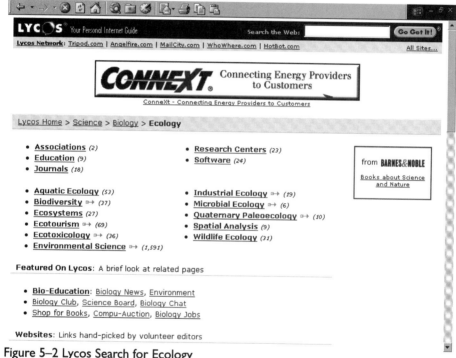

Figure 5–2 Lycos Search for Ecology

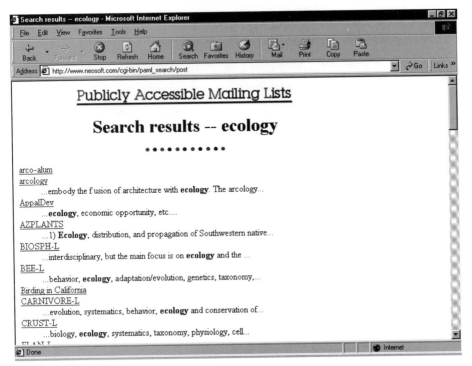

Figure 5–3 PAML Search for **Ecology**

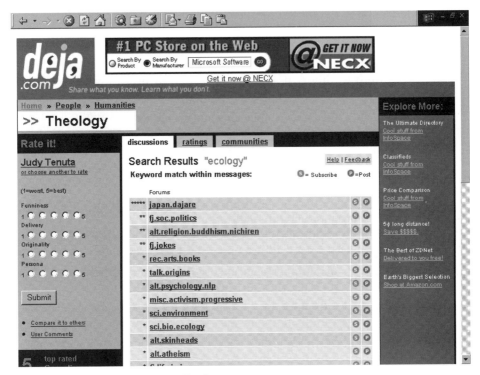

Figure 5–4 Deja.com Search for **Ecology**

DEVELOPING AN INTERNET RESOURCE GUIDE

What Is an Internet Resource Guide?

One way that librarians, information professionals, and subject experts are adding value to the networked information environment is through the development of subject-oriented Internet resource guides. For each guide, an author (or team of authors) scours the Internet for information on a particular topic and selects appropriate resources for inclusion. The author then organizes the information according to topic and/or format. Geographical and chronological organization schemes are also used when appropriate. The author may provide descriptive and evaluative information in addition to instructions for accessing the resources.

Hundreds of these guides, covering such diverse topics as children's literature, aerospace engineering, computer-mediated communication, and environmental law, are collected in the Argus Clearinghouse. Originally founded by Louis Rosenfeld (one of the authors of this book) while he was a librarian at the University of Michigan as the Clearinghouse for Subject-Oriented Internet Resource Guides, the clearinghouse has become a tremendously popular resource. Obviously there is a very real need in this environment for the value-added work that librarians and information professionals are well suited to perform.

People from all around the world develop these topical guides for a variety of reasons. First of all, when conducting Internet research for any reason it's very important to take good notes on where you go and what you find. To make this growing collection of notes more manageable, it helps to organize the information by topic or format, add descriptions, and format the references to each resource in a standard manner. Pretty soon your personal note taking evolves into a well-structured and fairly comprehensive guide to resources on your topic of interest. Why not make this guide available via the Internet so that others can benefit from your hard work? It's a great service to the Internet community and you might even earn fame within your field or area of interest.

Some librarians and subject specialists decide to make a guide available to their patrons via the Internet as an extension of their traditional collection development efforts. Others, like Susan, may work with a faculty member to design a guide around a college course, and then use that guide as a resource for teaching students how to use the Internet for research. Information professionals in corporate settings may develop a guide to useful resources for their sales or marketing or research departments. Alternatively, an organization may sponsor development of a guide that is designed to attract potential customers to their World Wide Web site. Whatever the reason, the development of a subject-oriented guide is an integral part of conducting Internet research.

Armed with dozens or even hundreds of resources, Susan is ready to begin developing her Internet resource guide. But make no mistake; there's still much work to be done. The process of transforming a raw list of resources into a well-developed guide is both time-consuming and intellectually challenging. But it makes all the difference in the world. Through the selection, description, evaluation, and organization of resources, a guide author shapes chaos into order. The resulting guide is a value-added information product that can really help people find the information they need.

The Design Process

When designing an Internet resource guide, it's important to balance form and function. On today's World Wide Web, the graphical capability and advertising often get in the way. Too many developers go for the flashy, high-impact graphics that may take forever to load. While aesthetics are important, primary consideration should be given to the usability of the guide. A modest graphic on the main page combined with a smaller graphic on all subsequent pages is usually sufficient.

Several factors contribute to the usability of a guide. First of all, the foundation of a good guide is high-quality resource entries. Information about each resource should be presented in a consistent manner. Begin with meta information, or details about the resource. What is the title? How about the URL? Provide some keywords to suggest the content. Who maintains the resource? In addition to meta information, descriptive and evaluative information are very useful. Users need to know the subject matter of the resource, the intended audience, the quality and currency, the format, and how to access the information. The integration of hypertext links leading directly to the resources themselves is crucial.

Attributes of an Effective Internet Resource Guide

- High-quality resource entries
- Consistent presentation
- Clear page layout
- Logical architecture: categories, levels, hierarchies

Having developed the information about each resource, it's time for Susan to design the template for her resource pages. To avoid long pages that are slow to load, it's best to put each resource description on its own page. A nice page layout allows users to scan the meta information, descriptions, and evaluations quickly. Try to avoid forcing the user to scroll down the page to find important information. Consider employing navigational aids, such as Back to the Main Page links, so that users can move around easily and efficiently. It's very easy to get lost when exploring hypertextual documents. Navigational aids can provide the context necessary to maintain a sense of place.

With the individual pages taken care of, Susan turns her efforts to the architectural design of the guide. The most important architectural decision relates to the use of organization schemes. A topical organization scheme is almost always called for, but don't stop there. Organizing the resources by format can also be very useful. A user may only be looking for software programs, journals, or discussion groups. Certain topic areas lend themselves to chronological or geographical organization.

One the nicest qualities of hypertext is that it supports multiple pathways to the same information. Susan begins with a topical organization scheme. She reviews the resources that she's collected, and begins to sort them into logical categories. Coming up with those categories is not always easy. Looking at the way others have organized similar resources can often be helpful. A white board or set of index cards can also be useful in facilitating this iterative process. When developing organizational schemes, key questions relate to the breadth and depth. How many categories should there be? How many subcategories? How many levels in the hierarchy? Well, there are no definitive answers to these questions, but human-computer interface studies have suggested that menus should include no more than 12 categories (breadth) and hierarchies should have no more than three levels (depth). As hierarchies go beyond these limits, it becomes increasingly difficult for users to find what they're looking for.

PUBLICITY, FEEDBACK, AND REDESIGN

By following some basic principles of design, Susan has developed a useful and usable guide. However, she needs to complete one more step in the process before being ready to turn the guide over to the biology students. Susan should now publicize her guide to some of the Internet communities it covers. People in those communities will probably be very appreciative of her efforts. They are also the best source for feedback on the guide. Susan posts messages to each community announcing the rough draft of her guide. She asks people to take a look and let her know what they think. Some tell her of useful resources that she has missed. Others provide suggestions for enhancing the overall design of the guide. Still others simply thank her for developing such a useful resource. Susan saves the latter messages, incorporates the suggestions, and announces the finished version of the guide. In addition to posting messages to the ecology-related communities on the Internet, Susan submits her guide for inclusion in a number of Internet directories and virtual libraries. She also submits it for indexing by several of the major search tools. Now the guide will be available not only to the biology students at her university but to anyone interested in ecology anywhere in the Internet community.

Susan's research project illuminates the iterative and interactive nature of Internet research. It began with the use of virtual libraries, Internet directories, search engines, and online communities of people, and culminated in the development of a subject-oriented guide. No single tool or type of tool could have helped her identify all of the resources she found during her search. By finding clues and following leads, Susan collected a substantial variety of resources. By selecting, describing, organizing, and evaluating resources from that collection, Susan developed a useful guide. Finally, by publicizing the availability of her guide to appropriate communities, Susan made it more readily accessible. However, Susan's

> Most of the tools covered in this second edition did not exist two years ago, were in rudimentary form, or have metamorphosed from very simple beginnings into something rich and strange.

work does not end here. The rapid pace of change on the Internet ensures that guides quickly become obsolete without constant updates. Some resources will disappear and new ones will take their place. New formats incorporating interactive video and virtual reality technology will become increasingly prevalent. Old formats will slide into obscurity.

The same will happen with the tools for conducting Internet research. Most of the tools covered in this second edition did not exist two years ago, were in rudimentary form, or have metamorphosed from very simple beginnings into something rich and strange. How many of today's tools will exist two years from now? What types of advanced tools will take their place? It's impossible to predict all of the twists and turns to come, but certain developments seem inevitable. The quantity of Internet information will continue to grow exponentially. The tools will become more powerful and sophisticated. Humans will continue to play an important role in the identification, selection, description, evaluation, and organization of information. And the process of conducting research via the Internet will remain challenging, interesting, and rewarding.

Chapter Six

Online Communities as Tools for Research and Reference

**Louis B. Rosenfeld, revised
by GraceAnne A. DeCandido**

The explosion of virtual communities has made them a fixture in our culture. We see references to them in the media and make references to them in our lives on a daily basis. The communities may be virtual, but they have a cyber-reality no less real for being "cyber." And they have their unspoken assumptions and guidelines, just like other kinds of communities.

COMMUNITIES IN GENERAL: A TWO-WAY STREET

One reason that communities get started is because some individuals discover that they have something in common, such as geography or a mutual interest. But that's only part of the picture. A community is kind of like a bank: members make withdrawals, but they also have to leave deposits. For example, if you wish to be a part of a community centered in a neighborhood, you'll enjoy a number of benefits, such as familiar faces to greet as you walk down the street, or someone to feed your cat when you go on vacation. But you'll also find yourself mowing an elderly neighbor's lawn or keeping a watchful eye on the local kids playing in the neighborhood. So belonging to a community requires give and take.

Online communities are wonderful, perhaps unequaled information sources. On the other hand, they're often as inconsistent and undependable as people. The best approach to leveraging the expertise of an online community is to demonstrate your willingness to contribute as well as receive information. This chapter will explain why this is the case; it will also familiarize you with the basics of online communities and how you can use them as sources of information.

THE ONLINE COMMUNITY

An online community is a group of individuals who share and exchange communications regarding a common interest by using information technology. The community can range in size from two people to thousands. Their communications are generally one-to-many; in other words, when an individual communicates, all other members of that community receive or can access that communication. Online communities, unlike most physical ones, are centered on topics rather than geographic locales. The community's shared interest can range from alternative medicine to Yiddish theater to the merits of living in San Francisco; in effect, any topic that is of interest to more than one person on the planet. And a number of information technologies are used to support communities—the most popular are the various programs that support electronic mailing lists (popularly known as "listserves") and Usenet newsgroups, described on pages 78–80, titled "Common Tools for Online Communities."

WHY USE ONLINE COMMUNITIES?

This book describes many resources for searching besides online communities: virtual libraries, directories, and search engines. All are valuable in some situations, less so in others; none are particularly adept at handling all information needs. Online communities are obviously a bit different from these other resources, as they require you to interact with other Internet users to gather the information you need. This process of interacting with others is very time-consuming; first you'll need to find an appropriate online community, then get to know its culture to some degree, and finally ask your question. Maybe you'll get some answers right away, maybe you'll get none at all. Perhaps some answers will need clarification, which will add a few more iterations to the process. And don't forget the trials of (mis)communication: as with any interaction, things can and often do go wrong. You want to make sure that you don't start off on the wrong foot when you post your first question to an online community. And even if you exercise the utmost care in posting your question, the current volume of traffic on the list may reduce the probability of its attracting a response to almost nil.

So why on earth would you use an online community as a source of information? Because humans are without a doubt the best information filters. They can and often will help you in ways that none of the other resources, all of which are automated, ever will. For example, a person is daily exposed to information from so many different sources: newspapers, books, radio, gossipy acquaintances, television, passersby, even dreams. No piece of software can keep up with all these sources, but many of the people you encounter in online communities will be able to summon almost instantaneously a fact or a pointer from these sources to help answer your question, no matter how disjointed it might be.

People will be able to understand something about you and the context of your information need. They'll know to give you a different answer if you're a college professor than if you were nine years old. They will also be adept at handling the ambiguity that is inherent in language. Unlike most software programs, people will understand that if you're looking for statistics about a pitcher, you're not talking about something to pour water from. And ultimately, people often enjoy helping each other; if you pose your question the right way, solving it may serve as an interesting and entertaining challenge for members of an online community. We hope this chapter will equip you to understand online communities better and to ask your question the "right way."

WHEN TO USE ONLINE COMMUNITIES

Online communities aren't usually appropriate sources for answers to quick, ad hoc questions (see exceptions, such as Stumpers, noted on page 76). If anything, you'll annoy the members of those communities by bugging them with queries that you likely could have answered by spending just a few minutes doing the research yourself. Besides, who's to say they'll get right back to you with an answer quickly? Rely on online communities when you're truly stuck, when you want to do in-depth and qualitative searching, and when time isn't a major factor. Here are some basic rules of thumb to keep in mind when considering querying an online community. Use them when:

- *you're not in a hurry to get an answer*: As mentioned above, it can take a lot of time for you to find an appropriate online community and properly post your question, much less receive an answer.

- *you're completely stuck*: If you can demonstrate to a community that you've tried to answer the question yourself, you'll likely be able to enlist others who see the seriousness of your efforts.
- *you need to do exhaustive research and want to turn over every stone*: You could use every search engine, virtual library, and directory available and still not find some resources others may already know about. Additionally, you may learn "insider's information" about relevant resources that are under development and will be available soon.
- *you're hoping to get a good amount of descriptive information on resources*: While your Yahoo search will tell you that there's a wonderful-sounding archive of music lyrics, a person will not only tell you about that resource's scope, but also mention that it hasn't been accessible for the past four months.
- *you're hoping to get a good amount of evaluative information on resources*: Similarly, people will steer you clear of substandard resources and often provide a few words regarding the quality of a resource. If you get enough responses, you'll find that you have in effect conducted an "opinion poll," and comparing the answers might be very informative.
- *the product of your search is intended to serve a broad audience*: If you are eventually going to make the results of your search widely available, announce that along with your question. It makes sense to enlist the eventual beneficiaries of your hard work in the searching process.

There are also some listserves specifically designed to answer queries. One of these is Stumpers, for difficult reference questions. Stumpers is meant to be a court of last resort, but it is also used by librarians and researchers who are asked questions out of their area of expertise or out of the scope of their collections. Stumpers has an extensive archive that should be searched before any query is posted. Stumpers maintains both unofficial and official Web pages (the former at *www.du.edu/~penrosel/wombat/index.html*, run by T. F. Mills, and the latter at *www.cuis.edu/~stumpers/*, run by the rotating student-moderator at Dominican University's Graduate School of Library and Information Science

---

Stumpers—for difficult reference questions

Archives: *www.cuis.edu/~stumpers/*

To post a query: stumpers-l@crf.cuis.edu

[GLIS]). E-mail questions to stumpers-l@crf.cuis.edu, following the in-dicated guidelines.

WHAT TO LOOK FOR IN AN ONLINE COMMUNITY

Appropriate people and quality information are the hallmarks of the right online community for your needs. It seems that almost every day we hear of a new resource designed to help users search for mailing lists and newsgroups. (See Chapter Nine for more details.) Finding relevant online communities is obviously important and necessary, but is only half of the battle. You'll also want to determine which of those communities are actually *appropriate*. Posting to an inappropriate community will sim-ply be a waste of your time and that community's time.

So what's an appropriate community? Ideally, it should fit the follow-ing criteria:

- *traffic levels shouldn't be too high*: Your query is competing with all the other queries posted to that community. Will anyone even notice your posting if it's just one of 100? Or even 30? A lot de-pends on the level of traffic that is normal for the list. At the other extreme, some communities are seemingly inactive and have no, or very few, new postings. Does it make sense to post to such a group? Surprisingly, yes—a fair number of "lurkers" may still sub-scribe; they may be quite happy to help you, because your query may be interesting enough to reinvigorate their community's dis-cussion. Knowledge of your community's habits is as crucial here as anywhere else: for some communities, dozens of queries a day aren't excessive, while for others, a handful is all it takes to bog things down.
- *the community's topic should be as narrow and specific as possible*: Let's say your query has something to do with Welsh history, and your choices of online communities include ones that deal with Welsh history and British history. While it may be tempting to post to both, the British online history community probably has higher traffic levels and fewer Welsh history experts than the Welsh his-tory community. And the folks who do happen to subscribe to both communities will come across your posting twice, which might an-noy some. So at least start by posting to the Welsh community, and if you have no luck there, come back to the British community, mention your lack of luck with the other group, and ask there.
- *the community should be supportive of questions*: Spend some time (a few weeks if you can spare it) "lurking" or listening in on the

discussion in a given online community. Do members "flame" the folks asking questions (that is, send derogatory or angry messages)? If they do, it's probably not worth bothering to post your question. Do they often mention a useful FAQ (a document containing answers to frequently asked questions)? If they do, you ought to check that before asking your question. Do they seem to favor one type of question over another? If so, emulate the former. In general, your common sense will be your best guide here.

- *the community should be capable of assisting with questions*: Do the answers to other folks queries seem to be helpful? Do the discussants generally seem competent, or do they come off as uninformed or just plain reckless in their answers? You may find that, based on the limited searching you have already done, you have become *the* expert on your area of interest relative to the folks in

COMMON TOOLS FOR ONLINE COMMUNITIES

If you're new to Internet communities, you'll want to understand a bit about their underlying technologies and their relative advantages and disadvantages. Here are a few things you should know regarding the major tools for using online communities.

Mailing lists and Usenet newsgroups cover a limitless number of topics. Both types of tools are free to "subscribers" and are fairly easy to use; therefore, it's not surprising how popular they are. You'll find a lot of variety in both mailing lists and newsgroups: levels of discussion vary from highly scholarly or serious to completely sophomoric and meaningless; community spirit can range from warm-and-fuzzy to supportive to indifferent to downright nasty; and traffic volumes may range from one posting per month to 100 per day. This wide variety is due to a number of factors, including the nature of the topic, its audience, the age of the mailing list or newsgroup, and whether its postings are "moderated" or controlled by an individual who has been entrusted with this responsibility. Generally, the postings you'll find on mailing lists tend to be informal in tone; questions, answers, group discussions, and arguments prevail, although you'll also encounter more official postings, such as conference announcements and press releases.

Electronic Mailing Lists

- *how they work*: Commonly known as "listserves," mailing lists are fueled by plain old electronic mail. Mailing list programs maintain lists of subscribers and their e-mail addresses; each mailing list has its own e-mail address, and when someone sends a message to that address, all the subscribers receive a copy of the posting. Although you may not realize that you're interacting with mailing list programs, it's helpful to recognize a few of the popular "brand names": Listserv, Mailserv, Majordomo, and Listproc are all a little different, but basically do the same things. E-mail is used to subscribe and unsubscribe to a mailing list, to customize one's subscription to a mailing list, and to post and receive mailing list postings. Every posting from a mailing list will end up in your electronic mailbox, along with all your other mail. There are thousands of open mailing lists available today, many of them categorized at Liszt (see Chapter Two).

- *benefits*: Due to their reliance on widely accepted and common electronic mail technologies, mailing lists are easy to use; if you can use e-mail, you can use a mailing list. Because many of the mailing list technologies come directly from academia, participants are more likely to be "serious academics." Therefore, discussion levels are usually a little more serious than those found on Usenet newsgroups, and it's more likely that a mailing list is moderated or filtered. Mailing list software programs generally provide for archiving their postings, so you can often search for information that may have been posted months or years ago.
- *disadvantages*: It can be intrusive to find mail addressed to a group mixed in with the personal mail in your mailbox, especially if your mailer cannot sort mail for you by topic or sender. It can be really irritating to find 50 or 100 of these postings in your mailbox some morning, especially if the topic of discussion isn't your cup of tea. As a solution, some mailing lists can be set to combine each day's worth of postings into one long message called a "digest" that gets mailed once daily. However, digests are less interactive and reduce the timeliness of receiving postings to once per day. The interface and commands for doing anything aside from receiving and posting mailing list messages (e.g., searching an archive or setting your subscription to "digest") are quite awkward.

Usenet Newsgroups

- *how they work*: Much like individual mailing lists, each Usenet newsgroup covers a specific topic. You need to actively access Usenet postings from your Web browser, as opposed to passively receiving e-mailed postings from mailing lists. You can subscribe to, view, and post to specific newsgroups from a Web browser such as Netscape or Internet Explorer. When you access a newsgroup, you'll usually first see an index of all the postings submitted since you last checked. You'll be able to select the specific posting you want to read and easily ignore the others. You may also view a related subset of a newsgroup's postings, called "threads"; monitoring an individual thread is akin to listening in on one conversation at a cocktail party and ignoring the others in the room. Depending on the policies of your Internet Service Provider, usually only the most recent one or two weeks of Usenet newsgroup postings are archived, so if you don't check your news within that period, you might miss out on some postings.

- *benefits*: News readers allow you to sift through many postings in a single session without cluttering your electronic mailbox. Additionally, threaded news readers enable you to keep up with the interesting discussions going on in a newsgroup while easily ignoring the others. It's much easier to determine the topics of newsgroups than with mailing lists, as Usenet follows a fairly standard convention for naming newsgroups.
- *disadvantages*: You'll find that the levels of traffic and quality of discussion on newsgroups tend to vary more widely than in mailing lists. If you don't access newsgroups through the Web, you also have to set up and master yet another piece of software.

Newsgroups, Listserves, Spam, and Ads

Spam and ads have become facts of online life. When you join online mailing lists or newsgroups, you and your mailbox may become subject to spams. A spam is an e-mail message, sent to a targeted group of people, advertising—usually in an obnoxious manner—some product or service. These messages may also be either "get-rich-quick" schemes or offers of pornographic material. While intrusive and annoying, they can be dealt with by judicious use of the Delete key. Just as having a street mailing address and subscribing to a magazine may subject you to paper junk mail ads, having an e-mail address allows the possibility of unwanted online ads. Newsgroup posters can be particularly afflicted with this kind of advertising, so be aware of the possibility.

HOW TO ASK YOUR QUESTION

Perhaps your biggest challenge lies in getting someone to answer your question. If you come off as an Internet "newbie," or as someone with no sense of the culture of the specific online community, you're likely to be ignored. If you don't follow some basic rules of "netiquette," you might be laughed at or flamed. And if you don't time your posting well, many members of the online community may never even notice that you submitted it. Following are some common sense dos and don'ts to help you avoid some of the pitfalls along the path to successful queries.

- *do keep your message brief and clear*: We live in times of short attention spans; long postings are simply fodder for Delete keys. Be as clear as possible, though, about what you need.
- *do identify yourself*: Many ignore all postings from anonymous or pseudonymous names. Use your real name, your city and state, and, if you have a title that's short and readily comprehensible, add that too. If you are a college student, list your university affiliation. Some argue that students should never admit that they are, actually, students, or people will flame them assuming that they are only looking for homework help. Know your community, be honest with them, and if it is for homework help, say so!
- *do state where else you are posting your request*: This is good netiquette, allowing readers who may chance upon your posting a second or third time to easily ignore it.
- *do state your goals*: People will be more likely to help you if you give them a little context for your query; if you can, let them know why you're looking for the information, how you'll use it, and who will benefit from it.
- *do tell them what you already know*: It's important to show that you've done at least some of your homework, so some quick and dirty searching before you post is in order. Besides, you don't really want to get 20 responses describing the obvious or popular resources. You want to know about the resources that are hard to find or that aren't up and running just yet.
- *do ask for the addresses of knowledgeable people*: Finding and befriending a few experts out there will make your life much easier. And having a referral ("so-and-so from such-and-such mailing list gave me your name and suggested that I contact you") will go a long way to break down the expert's defenses.
- *don't ever announce that you're a novice in the area*: Doing so may reduce the likelihood of a response. And if you do receive a response that isn't clear to you, ask the individual poster for clarification, or show the message to a local expert or friend who might be able to offer an explanation.
- *don't use long and silly signature files*: You should project a seri-

ous image for yourself and your query, so, for example, including a large Bart Simpson graphic in your sigfile won't help your cause.

- *do be prepared to repeat your request periodically*: Sometimes you simply won't get any responses no matter what you do. Consider making your preliminary results available so the community can see that you're actually working on it. This will also provide them with another chance to give you feedback.

This last point recalls our initial discussion about the two-way nature of communities. If you are extensively researching a topic, providing a summary of the results of your search can be a great enticement for members of an online community to respond and help you. As they are already Internet users, they understand how difficult it is to find relevant, useful information. If you portray yourself as one willing to do this work, you will find much more interest (and general encouragement) than if you had simply asked a question without offering up your results.

We hope that this chapter demonstrates the value of the expertise found in online communities, and helps you to formulate queries effective at unlocking that expertise.

Chapter Seven

Virtual Libraries

Peter Morville, revised
by GraceAnne A. DeCandido

Virtual libraries, or value-added collections of Internet resources, are among the more civilized areas of an otherwise chaotic and unruly cyberspace. Although a far cry from the order and stability of traditional libraries, virtual libraries do provide a taste of the value that librarians can add to the Internet through the application of traditional skills in a wildly nontraditional environment. Through the identification, selection, organization, description, and evaluation of Internet information resources, "digital librarians" or "cybrarians" create virtual libraries that help people find information, software, and communities of people. Virtual libraries typically provide an organizational hierarchy with topical categories for browsing. Some provide a query interface to allow keyword or full-text searching. Some virtual libraries are maintained by a single organization while others are supported through the volunteer efforts of people around the world.

The human role in the development and maintenance of virtual libraries also leads to their primary weakness. Compared with Internet directories, for instance, virtual libraries are relatively limited in the number of topics they cover. The quality and depth of coverage often varies widely from topic to topic. In addition, virtual libraries cannot compete in the area of currency. With a few exceptions, virtual libraries are almost totally supported by the efforts of volunteers. It is impossible for these people to keep up with the exponential growth of Internet information resources.

SEARCHING TIPS

Virtual libraries are best for conducting research but can also be useful for answering reference questions. Whatever the nature of the query, it's usually easiest to begin by browsing through the organizational hierarchy. This is typically the shortest path to a guide or Web site on a given topic. If you don't find anything by browsing, try the search capability. You may find a guide that leads you directly to a useful resource, or a related resource within a guide which then leads you to a useful resource.

CONSIDERATIONS FOR THE FUTURE

We live in an information age with vast oceans of data at our fingertips. Unfortunately, finding useful information can be as difficult as finding a needle in a haystack. Automated search engines and directories can help, but only so much. Human efforts to identify, describe, organize, and evaluate information resources are an essential component of the solution.

To address the limitations of virtual libraries, a number of organizations are exploring an economic model, namely content-driven advertising, which provides a financial incentive for the development and maintenance of top-quality virtual libraries. Once this model proves itself, we can expect to see dramatic improvements in the scope, depth, currency, and overall quality of virtual libraries.

As the volume of Internet information continues to grow, users will increasingly turn to the value-added virtual libraries for fast and easy access to Internet information resources. The future of virtual libraries holds great promise.

A FORMER DEVELOPER'S PERSPECTIVE: WILLIAM F. ZIMMERMAN

In mid-1993, when Zimmerman began thinking about the Internet Book Information Center, there were only 130 World Wide Web sites. By June 1995, Publishers Weekly called Zimmerman's site "the granddaddy of book-related sites on the Internet." He no longer maintains this site. Here are Zimmerman's puckish and occasionally sardonic thoughts on where things have gone since then.

As I write in September 1998, the essay I wrote for the first edition of this book seems rather quaint. The function of virtual librarianship still remains important and vital, and the virtual librarian still faces conceptual, technical, and spiritual challenges—but the context surrounding the task has changed dramatically.

An entertaining way to explore those challenges in today's environment is to examine the work of the "poster boy" for virtual librarianship, Matt Drudge. Of course, I call Drudge a role model for virtual librarians with my tongue in cheek, but only partly. Drudge got his start as a primitive virtual librarian in the Neolithic era of the Web, and even today his site (*www.drudgereport.com*) still bears many of the decorative motifs of the Web's cave dwellers. Consider:

- He maintains a "laundry list" of links to other content providers.
- He communicates with a community via a mailing list.
- He provides a modest amount of homegrown content and a generous helping of point of view.

Drudge earned his success by meeting the conceptual, technical, and spiritual challenges of virtual librarianship head on. He found an unoccupied conceptual niche—"prenews" or "news about news" and filled it better than the existing, heavily capitalized traditional media players. He settled on a simple editorial and technical model which apparently requires very little in the way of advanced technology—just HTML links and a mailing list—and scales up well: the more gossip is sent his way, the more appealing he can make his service. He provided a unique point of view that resonated with many people—a "Walter Winchell" model of sensationalism mixed with half-baked substance. Of course, it is in this spiritual dimension that Drudge justly receives his sharpest criticism. Lightning struck caveman Matt Drudge, and he is now the most famous virtual librarian on the planet, with millions of readers coming to his cave every day. As Drudge's story illustrates, resources and even skill alone are not the determining factor in making a virtual library a roaring success. Despite his shortcomings in capital and in skills, and a questionable spiritual basis for his work, he had a strong concept—a "metalibrary" for unproven political and entertainment gossip (why didn't I think of that?)—that proved robust and timely.

Being a virtual librarian at this moment in the Web's history is like living in an underdeveloped economy where most people labor mightily, and worthily, with all the skills at their command but are unable to get past sustenance living. Most virtual librarians are undercapitalized; a few are overcapitalized. Members of the undercapitalized majority work diligently to serve the needs of their particular community, but they must always scrap for time and resources. On the overcapitalized end of the spectrum of "virtual librarianship" are enterprises, such as About.com, that are trying to apply mass production techniques to artisan's work, with unproven business models and, as might be expected, moderate but not overwhelming success. On the whole, Web virtual libraries whose scalability is gated by human editorial resources have not been conspicuous winners in the race to develop viable business models.

A few exceptional virtual librarians, like Drudge, combine luck, skill, and strategy to become noteworthy figures in the New Economy; but there is no great middle class of virtual librarians at this date. One might say that the pioneering members of the middle class for virtual librarians—the Booker T. Washingtons of their day—are the "staff ontologists" at Yahoo, who have the right combination of tools, visibility, and simplicity to provide instant, self-help, "virtual library" reference services for millions of customers every day. Similarly, librarians and information professionals often perform virtual library tasks as integral parts of their "day jobs." But for most of us, the day has not yet come when virtual librarianship is a career path in itself. For now, the decision to build and maintain a virtual library must be a carefully considered one, focusing on the conceptual and spiritual issues: can I define something worthwhile to do? Am I going to be happy doing it as a part-time project? We eagerly await the day when a viable business model makes it possible for us to cry, like Dr. Martin Luther King, "Free at last! Thank God Almighty, free at last!"

ARGUS AND THE INTERNET PUBLIC LIBRARY

The first two virtual libraries we will look at are the Argus Clearinghouse, and the Internet Public Library. Argus is the professional home of two authors of the first edition of this book, Peter Morville and Louis Rosenfeld. Its third original author, Joseph Janes, is the founder of the Internet Public Library.

ARGUS CLEARINGHOUSE

Meta Information

URL:	*www.clearinghouse.net/index.html*
Resource Type:	World Wide Web site
Use:	finding information resources, software, and online communities; primarily useful for research but may help with some reference queries; best for finding a variety of useful resources under a broad heading
Navigation:	browse subject hierarchy
Scope:	broad with the following top-level categories: Arts & Humanities, Business & Employment, Communication, Education, Engineering, Environment, Government & Law, Health & Medicine, Places & Peoples, Recreation, Science & Mathematics, Social Sciences & Social Issues
Volume:	1,350+ topical guides; note that each guide contains dozens or hundreds of resources
Searching Tips:	select a broad category and scan the guide titles
Strengths:	certain topics covered extremely well, excellent organizational schemes; each guide submitted is evaluated and over 90 percent are rejected, so quality is high
Weaknesses:	sparse coverage of some topics, variable quality from guide to guide, inability to perform global searches
Updates:	new guides and new versions of guides are added once or twice per month; updates to the guides themselves are dependent on the authors and vary from guide to guide
Questions:	Louis Rosenfeld, lou@argus-inc.com

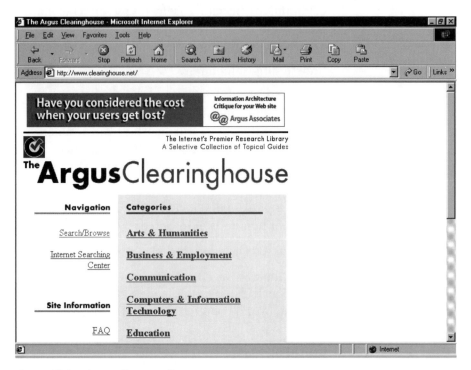

Figure 7–1   Argus Opening Page

Description

The Argus Clearinghouse (Figure 7–1) is a collection of subject-specific guides that provide intellectual access to thousands of Internet information resources. Topics covered range from philosophy to personal finance to neuroscience. The guides provide objective descriptions and subjective evaluations as well as instructions for accessing the resources. The clearinghouse collocates guides developed and maintained by authors on remote servers all over the world. Currently, the clearinghouse includes guides in plain text and/or hypertext formats.

Evaluation

The major strengths of the Argus Clearinghouse stem from a firm embrace of the value-added approach and a distributed model for online publishing. By encouraging authors all over the world, many of whom are subject specialists, to develop value-added guides that identify, select, organize, describe, and evaluate Internet information resources, the clearinghouse takes advantage of the capabilities for communication and collaboration via the Internet and taps the skills, knowledge, and energy of willing individuals on a global scale. Some of the top guides serve as the single best source of Internet-based information on a particular subject. If you're planning a comprehensive search on a specific topic, the clearinghouse is a great place to start. If a guide on that topic exists, much of your work may already be done.

Sample Search

Objective: Shaniqua would like to find some general information about art museum resources on the Internet.

From the Argus main menu, with its 13 general subject areas, she selects Arts & Humanities (Figure 7–2). That category takes her to a subcategory list that includes Museums and Galleries as well as Visual Arts. Moving to Museums and Galleries, Shaniqua can choose either Art Galleries and Museums or Exhibitions. Art galleries and museums provides her with a list of five resources, all rated with Argus's system of check marks (one to five checks for each of five criteria, which are then averaged). Choosing World Wide Arts Resources, which has the top rating of five checks, she gets to a page that lists the site's URL, keywords, compiler, rating, and—a definite plus—the most recent date that Argus staff checked the site. She then can connect to the site itself, with a great deal of information about it already in hand.

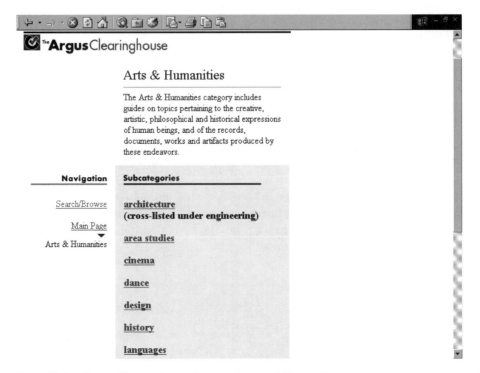

Figure 7–2   Argus Clearinghouse List on Arts and Humanities

INTERNET PUBLIC LIBRARY

Meta Information

URL: *www.ipl.org*

Resource Type: World Wide Web site

Use: finding the most useful and interesting information resources, software, and online communities on a particular topic; useful for reference and research; asking online reference questions; opening page lists Resource of the Week and Site of the Moment with links and brief commentary

Navigation: browse using traditional library metaphor, browse subject hierarchy, search using keywords, ask for help

Scope: broad, with the following top-level categories: Reference, Arts & Humanities, Business & Economics, Computers & Internet, Education, Entertainment and Leisure, Health & Medical Sciences, Law, Government & Political Science, Sciences & Technology, Social Sciences, Associations

Volume: includes IPL original resources, such as A+ Research & Writing for High School and College Students and also IPL Pathfinders

Searching Tips: browse the general categories; if that fails, try the keyword searching; as a last resort, submit an online reference question

Strengths: well-organized, resources of consistent high quality, interactive reference component

Weaknesses: limited number of topics and resources

Updates: variable

Questions: ipl@ipl.org

Submissions: *www.ipl.org/ref/RR/recommend.html*

NOTE: The Internet Public Library (Figure 7–3) has a mirror site at the University of Lund, in Sweden (*http://ipl.ub.lu.se/*).

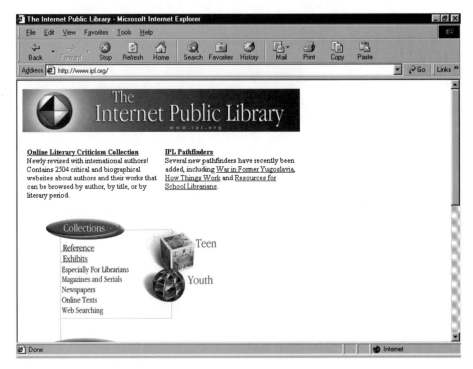

Figure 7–3   Home Page of the Internet Public Library *www.ipl.org/*

Description

The Internet Public Library (IPL) is more than just a virtual library. Using a metaphor for a traditional library, the IPL is organized into a number of divisions including Reference, Youth, and Librarian Services. For the purposes of this book, we are concerned primarily with the Reference department. The Internet Public Library expands on the value-added concept by bringing online reference librarians into the picture. Questions can be submitted using online forms, e-mail, or an object-oriented multiuser environment which facilitates real-time interaction between librarians and patrons. The Internet Public Library also provides a Ready Reference section that meets our standard definition of a virtual library. The Ready Reference section provides topical categories for browsing and a query interface for keyword searching. Pursuing the goal of fast and easy access to information, the IPL includes a limited set of high-quality resources. In addition to direct links, descriptive, evaluative information is provided for each resource.

Evaluation

The Ready Reference section of the Internet Public Library is an excellent tool for quickly finding a few high-quality resources on a given topic. It is one of the best places to go on the Internet if you are looking for a specific answer to a factual question. A well-designed organization scheme combines with the keyword searching tool to allow for fast, easy access to information.

Sample Search

Objective: Paul would like to find some free stock quote services.

From the main menu of Reference, Paul can browse through the subject categories or search by keywords. First, he decides to try the query interface which allows him to perform Boolean searches and to specify author and subject category fields. Paul enters **stocks** into the general query box and is rewarded with 12 hits (Figure 7–4). He browses the results, which provide title, author, keywords, and a brief description for each resource, and he finds a couple of stock quote services. Returning to the main Reference menu, he browses through the subject categories and selects Business and Economics. He then browses through several subcategories, chooses Finance and then Investments and finds about 20 resources, closer in scope to what he is looking for. Both the browsing and searching capabilities provide fast and easy access to the

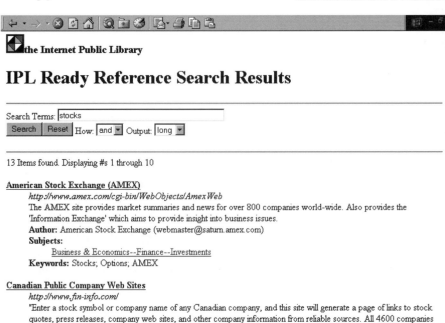

Figure 7–4   Internet Public Library Search for **Stocks**

resources. Paul decides to ask an IPL reference librarian whether any European or Japanese stock quote services are available on the Internet. He can choose whether to submit his question via e-mail or an online form. Within a few hours, an IPL librarian responds via e-mail with a couple of interesting services to try out.

MAGELLAN INTERNET DIRECTORY

Meta Information

URL: *magellan.excite.com/*

Resource Type: World Wide Web site

Use: finding information resources and online commu-
                     nities; primarily useful for research but may also help
                     with some reference queries

Navigation: browse the subject hierarchy; search the full text of
                     resource titles and descriptions

Scope: broad, with the following top-level categories: Au-
                     tos, Business, Careers, Computers, Education, En-
                     tertainment, Games, Health, Home, Horoscopes,
                     Lifestyle, News, People & Chat, Reference, Rela-
                     tionships, Shopping, Sports, and Travel

Searching Tips: take advantage of the Boolean capabilities (AND,
                     OR, NOT); proximity, adjacency, and stemming are
                     also possible; it can also be useful to limit by cat-
                     egory or minimum rating

Strengths: descriptions, evaluations, and ratings for each re-
                     source; only the most interesting resources for each
                     category; a powerful search interface combined with
                     a well-designed subject hierarchy

Figure 7–5   Magellan Internet Directory Opening Page

Description

The Magellan Internet Guide (despite its name and description as a search engine) is a virtual library that provides descriptions, evaluations, and ratings for a wide variety of Web sites, Usenet newsgroups, and electronic mailing lists (Figure 7–5). It is now a subsidiary of Excite, Inc. A distinguishing feature of Magellan is the evaluation scheme. Resources are evaluated using a one- to four-star rating system that takes into account coverage, organization, currency, and ease of access. Descriptions, intended audience, keywords, and other meta information are also provided. Users may browse through the subject hierarchy or search the full text of titles and resource descriptions and evaluations. Advanced search capabilities include Boolean logic (AND, OR, NOT), proximity and adjacency searching, and the use of wildcards for word stemming. Users can limit searching to reviewed sites, or to Green Light sites without any "content intended for mature audiences."

Evaluation

Magellan is a good resource for finding high-quality resources on a given topic. The topical hierarchy is well designed, the search interface is powerful yet easy to use, the search engine is fast, and the results are well presented. The integration of descriptions with an evaluation scheme makes Magellan a popular and useful tool. The labor necessary to review, describe, and evaluate each resource limits the numbers of resources that can be covered, however.

Sample Search

Objective: Edith would like to find some good genealogy resources.

Edith begins by browsing through the subject hierarchy with no luck. But when she searches **genealogy** and limits it to reviewed resources, she gets 410 hits, listed by relevance (Figure 7–6). The first is the Genealogy Home Page, (*www.genhomepage.com/*), a resource that lists over 2,700 links.

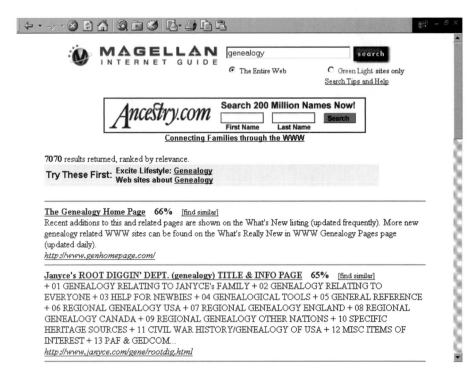

Figure 7–6   Magellan Search for **Genealogy**

WORLD WIDE WEB VIRTUAL LIBRARY

Meta Information

URL:	*vlib.org/Overview.html*
Resource Type:	World Wide Web site
Use:	finding information resources, software, and online communities; best for conducting research but may help with some reference queries; best for finding a variety of useful resources under a broad heading; most useful for queries that don't require current information
Navigation:	browse subject and resource type hierarchies, search full-text index
Scope:	broad, 14 top-level categories: Agriculture, Business and Economics, Computer Science, Communication and Media, Education, Engineering, Humanities, Information Management, International Affairs, Law, Recreation, Regional Studies, Science, Society
Searching Tips:	select a broad category and scan the section headings
Questions:	Gerard Manning, ger@vlib.stanford.edu

Description

The World Wide Web Virtual Library (VL) calls itself the oldest catalog of the Web, and it was started by Tim Berners-Lee, father of the Web (Figure 7–7). It is run by a loose confederation of volunteers, primarily at universities. Catalog pages are kept at Stanford University with mirror sites at Penn State, East Anglia, Geneva, and Argentina. As of July 30, 1999, the Web site had the following posted: "An adhoc committee is currently working on a proposal to create a formal structure for the Virtual Library, with a co-ordinating council and bylaws. The first set of bylaws were accepted by a membership vote in July of 1999, and a council to manage the central affairs of the VL is expected to be in place by October."

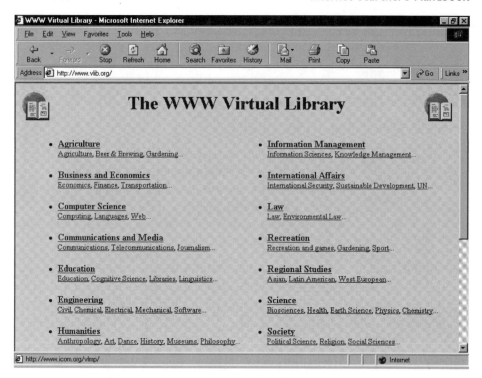

Figure 7–7   World Wide Web Virtual Library Opening Page

Sample Search

Objective: Carlo hopes to find some information about beer and beer making.

From the main menu, Carlo selects, under the general heading for Agriculture a subcategory for Beer and Brewing (Figure 7–8). That leads him to a page with links to everything from brewpubs and mail order beers to software, newsgroups, and regional guides.

Figure 7–8   The Beer Info Source, *http://www.beerinfo.com/vlib/index.html>*

ABOUT.COM

Meta Information

URL:	*www.about.com/*
Resource Type:	World Wide Web site
Use:	human guides—company-certified subject specialists—not only maintain the GuideSites but host live chats and manage bulletin board discussions on their topics
Navigation:	browse hierarchy; search resource titles
Scope:	top-level categories include Arts/Literature, Business/Careers, Computing/Technology, Education, Entertainment, Finance/Investing, Games, Health/Fitness, Hobbies, Home/Family, Internet/Online, Kids/Teens, Local, News/Media, Shopping, Society/Culture, Sports, and Travel
Volume:	600 guides on thousands of topics
Updates:	guides update sites weekly, sometimes daily
Questions:	reachus@about.com

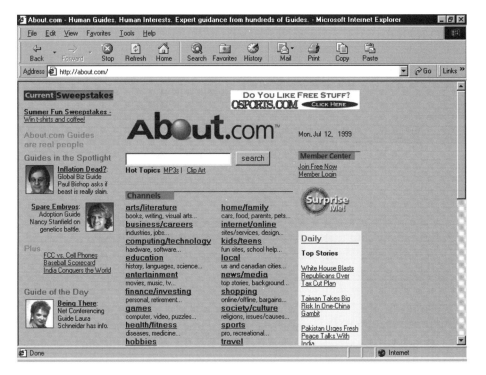

Figure 7–9   About.com Opening Page

Description

"We mine the Net so you don't have to" is the byline of About.com. Its site says that "hundreds" of people who are experts, fans, or otherwise passionate about a particular area are responsible for updating their topic sites weekly, although many do so daily. About.com stresses the reliability of its guides and its links (Figure 7–9). Some guides also produce online newsletters, site reviews, and other material for searchers, aficionados, and the curious.

Evaluation

About.com has attracted a lot of faithful adherents because it pulls together sites from all over the Web on chosen topics. It does save searching time if your interests coincide with one of its guides. While it may not be comprehensive, the quality is fairly strong.

Sample Search

Objective: Josh is looking for sites, particularly those with episode guides, to his favorite television show, *Buffy, the Vampire Slayer*.

Josh clicks on Entertainment on About.com's opening page, which brings him to TV and then to Historical/Fantasy Television, which has a guide, Elaine Hale. There, he finds links to Buffy and to other television shows that fit into the category, such as *Xena, Warrior Princess*. The Buffy links (Figure 7–10) include images, fan fiction, quotes from the show, chat archives, and information about the actors and their characters. He finds Buffy Cross and Stake at *http://slayer.simplenet.com/tbcs*, which includes detailed episode guides to the show, and has a Best of the Net designation.

Figure 7–10   From this page, select About.com Links for Buffy the Vampire Slayer

Chapter Eight

Internet Directories

Peter Morville, revised
by GraceAnne A. DeCandido

Internet directories or collections of resources maintained by the global Internet community are currently the most comprehensive, easy-to-use tools for finding Internet information. Consequently, they are the most popular. Yahoo, the best known tool in the category, has become a household name with its own quirky television commercials. Internet directories combine the features and capabilities of both virtual libraries and Internet search tools, balancing central control with distributed independence, and melding the efforts of human and machine.

Directories provide an organizational scheme to facilitate browsing. Topical, geographical, and alphabetical naming schemes are most common. The top levels of the organizational hierarchy are created by the managers of the directory. The creation of lower level categories is often left to the Internet community. Any person or business can "publish" information in these directories. For each resource, directories typically include only a title, although brief descriptive and evaluative information may also be presented. Many of the resource entries are provided by individuals or organizations who want to make sure that people will find their information. These information providers typically have control over the content of their descriptive and evaluative information and the location of their resource within the hierarchy, as long as they conform to a set of guidelines. Other resource entries are collected by automated search engines and intelligent agents that roam the Internet looking for new information resources. Preassigned keywords are used in the retrieval and organization of these resources. Depending on the directory, varying levels of editorial control are applied to resources submitted for inclusion by human users or electronic agents.

In addition to the organizational hierarchy, a query interface is typically provided to facilitate searching. The searching capabilities vary widely from directory to directory and may allow keyword, field specific, and/or full-text searching.

With several million potential contributors (some human and some machine), the strength of Internet directories clearly lies in their ability to be relatively comprehensive and up to date. The information in directories is made intellectually accessible through a varying combination of editorial control, placement within the organizational hierarchy, and the application of search capabilities. With a powerful search engine and flexible query interface, finding useful information resources can be fast and easy. At present, Internet directories are the premier tools for finding Internet information resources.

The weakness of Internet directories lies in the lack of editorial control over content and organization. The sheer volume of resources submitted for inclusion makes it virtually impossible for the directory managers to review each resource for quality, currency, and appropriateness within a given organizational category. They certainly don't have time to describe and evaluate each resource. These editorial duties are passed on to creators (who may or may not describe their own resources properly) or to automated processes. For this reason, a search in a directory may return a number of false drops and several low-quality or out-of-date resources. The burden for sifting through these pointers is placed on the user.

SEARCHING TIPS

Internet directories are useful for both reference and research. When you want a few useful resources on a given topic, the search capabilities of these directories are your best bet for fast, easy access. Try a specific term or keyword first and if that doesn't work, broaden your search. When you are conducting a more comprehensive research investigation, a combination of searching and browsing will serve you best.

A DEVELOPER'S PERSPECTIVE:
STEPHANIE WALKER

Stephanie Walker wrote about Galaxy in the first edition of this book. Here she describes for this edition the recent reinvention of the Galaxy Internet directory.

While the Internet is surely the first place many people look to find information, it can be the most frustrating resource to use because of the sheer volume of information it contains. There is no doubt about the wealth of information that is available. What is doubtful is how you will ever find what you are looking for.

Galaxy (*www.einet.net*) is the oldest Internet directory/search engine on the Internet. It was launched in January 1994 as a nonprofit venture and was one of the first directory services to join the WWW's hypertext capabilities with WAIS searching. In April 1995 Galaxy became a commercial service as part of TradeWave Corporation (formerly EINet). Unfortunately, all development of Galaxy ceased at the end of 1997, due to lack of funding. America's Health Network purchased Galaxy in September 1998 and Galaxy is once again adding more sites and topic areas each day.

Even with no marketing or promotion and very little funding in the past, Galaxy receives over 9,000 requests daily from sites wanting to be added. Each site is reviewed and placed in the topic area(s) where it belongs by a team of information professionals, most of whom hold master's degrees in library and information science. The topic hierarchy is constantly being evaluated and enhanced to enable users to browse the subjects that interest them.

Galaxy is a general Internet directory. The sites it contains can be divided into three basic categories: Academic, Commercial, and Social. These categories are further broken down into specific areas such as Poetry, Real Estate, and World Communities. Galaxy is the only directory to describe its entries by their format, such as:

- *Article:* A short, stand-alone text, usually about a single subject.
- *Announcement:* Describes an upcoming event.
- *Collection:* A set of stand-alone items. The items can be related, as in a collection of astronomy images, or the items can be unrelated, as in a museum, gallery, or general library. A collection implies that the items are stored and managed together.
- *Directory:* A guide to finding information, like the yellow pages of the phone book.

- *Product/Service Description*: A description of a product or service, including product catalogs.

Galaxy is searchable in two ways. First, users may simply browse through over 3,600 subject headings which are hierarchically arranged from broad to specific (Figure 8–1). This method works for users who are not exactly sure of what they are seeking. The second way to search Galaxy is by formulating search keywords and using the Boolean-based search engine. Galaxy allows users to search different parameters of the database. For example, users may search only the titles of sites within Galaxy, they may search the full text of those sites indexed in Galaxy, or they may search all of the links that are within each of those sites. These different methods of searching allow individuals to customize their search strategies to suit their needs exactly.

While they are not yet visible at the time this book is being written, we have created annotations for most of the sites listed in Galaxy to help users choose which links best meet their needs. The topic hierarchy of Galaxy is currently undergoing a massive restructuring that includes the development of more subject headings and cross references. Galaxy will continue to evolve as it gathers more sites that contain information about new subjects.

The process of indexing or imposing structure on the Internet is a part of the new frontier for information professionals. As such, it offers all of the excitement and aggravation of formulating new standards. Since there is no controlled vocabulary on the Internet, the task of organizing sites under subject headings is quite challenging and a bit overwhelming at times. Adding to this challenge is the huge number of sites that are being created daily on the Web. Each request from sites that want to be added to Galaxy is handled individually by a Galaxy Information Specialist who assigns it to the proper topic(s) according the established guidelines. Even with these guidelines, the process of classifying sites remains fairly subjective.

One of the classic indexing problems we have had to overcome is that many sites cannot easily be categorized under just one or two subject headings. For example, a commercial site may sell clothing, furniture, and sporting goods. All of these are consumer goods, but in order to index this site accurately, it must be listed at least three times. That takes more human and computer resources. Hence, Galaxy's extensive use of cross references. We want to provide as much access as possible without being too redundant and without using an excessive amount of resources. Therefore, an entry may be listed up to two or three times, but if it needs more than three subject headings, the cross references come into play.

Another challenging issue is that many individuals are creating their own home pages. These sites are full of sundry information, from what the creator had for dinner last night to excellent lists of links to sources on such specific topics as cancer research. It can be hard to decide to list a site under Cancer, for example, when half of the page is also dedicated to the creator's personal life, which may or may not have anything to do with cancer.

Like many information sources, Galaxy has also had to develop policies for dealing with sites that contain pornographic or illegal information as well as other controversial material. Since Galaxy is a private commercial entity, we are able to decide what kinds of sites we will and will not include in Galaxy. This type of selection is done by most Internet directories. Most directories will also only include sites deemed to have "valuable" information. Other directories only list sites that have paid to be listed there. Which of these directories is most useful will be determined by the type of information being sought by the individual user.

It is important to keep in mind that not all sites are listed in any one Internet directory or search engine. Some are more comprehensive than others. Some specialize in certain areas and cater to certain audiences. Users can best utilize Internet directories by learning good search strategies and by finding the right directory, or combination of directories, to search. As more and more people discover the Internet, directories and search engines, such as Galaxy, will continue to evolve and become better tools for weeding through the incredible amount of information that is now available online.

GALAXY

Meta Information

URL:	*www.einet.net/*or *www.galazy.com*
Resource Type:	World Wide Web site
Use:	finding information, software, and communities of people; useful for both reference and research
Navigation:	browse subject hierarchy; search category headings, resource titles, URLs, and full text
Scope:	broad, with the following top-level categories: Business and Commerce, Community, Engineering and Technology, Government, Humanities, Law, Leisure and Recreation, Medicine, Reference, Science, Social Sciences.
Searching Tips:	the extensive list of categories and subcategories is a good place to start; on the other hand, the query interface is quite flexible and easy to use, once you understand the field definitions (which can be displayed by selecting any of the hyperlinked field titles)
Updates:	daily
Questions:	staff@galaxy.com
Submissions:	*www.einet.net/annotate-help.html*

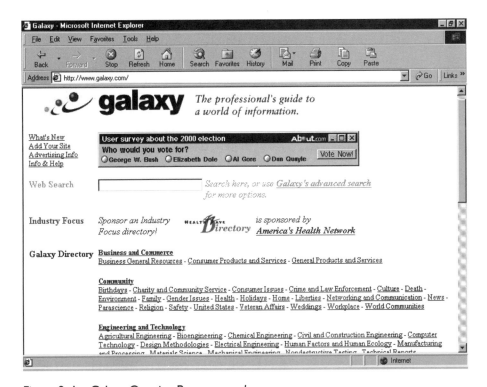

Figure 8–1   Galaxy Opening Page, *www.galaxy.com.*

Description

Galaxy is a subject-oriented directory of Internet information resources. Users can browse using the extensive subject hierarchy or search using the query interface. The query interface allows users to perform Boolean queries on the Galaxy navigational pages, the resource titles, the full text of referenced resources, and the hypertextual links in the referenced resources. Additionally, the interface still permits searching titles of gopher and telnet sites.

Evaluation

The advanced query interface enables searching the indexes of navigational pages, resource titles, full text, or hypertext, providing the experienced searcher with substantial flexibility and power. By experimenting with the interface, precision and recall can be manipulated to suit one's purposes. The capability of searching gopher and telnet indexes provides additional value. The subject hierarchy is well thought out and the page layout of the navigational pages is clean. There is no descriptive or evaluative information, however, to assist in making judgments about which resources to explore. Overall, Galaxy is a nicely designed navigational tool that should certainly be examined during any comprehensive research investigation and can also be quite useful for conducting reference.

Sample Search

Objective: Lara wants to find some information about hiking.

Using the subject hierarchy, Lara finds a link to Outdoor and Camping resources listed under Leisure and Recreation. From there, she finds several hiking directories and resources. A "see also" reference leads her to further hiking sites.

Using the query interface, Lara first tries searching the Galaxy navigational pages using **hiking** as her keyword (Figure 8–2). That produces over 170 hits, with options to refine her search, ranked in order of relevance. The first hit, with a score of 1,000, is Hiking Resources on the Internet, at (*www.gorp.com:80/gorp/activity/hiking.htm*).

To perform a comprehensive search, it's important for Lara to try all of the indices and the subject hierarchy.

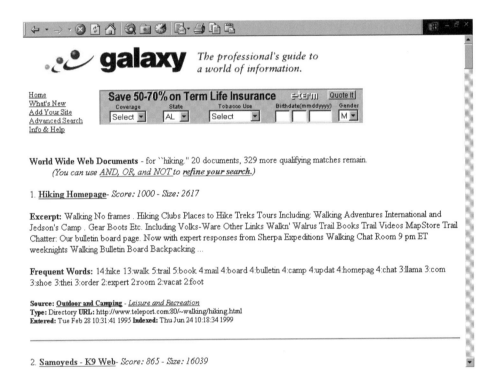

The professional's guide to a world of information.

galaxy

Home
What's New
Add Your Site
Advanced Search
Info & Help

Save 50-70% on Term Life Insurance e-term | Quote It|
Coverage   State   Tobacco Use   Birthdate(mmddyyyy)   Gender
[Select ▼]   [AL ▼]   [Select   ▼]   [   ][   ][   ]   [M ▼]

World Wide Web Documents - for "hiking." 20 documents, 329 more qualifying matches remain.
(You can use _AND, OR, and NOT_ to *refine your search.*)

1. Hiking Homepage- *Score: 1000 - Size: 2617*

Excerpt: Walking No frames . Hiking Clubs Places to Hike Treks Tours Including: Walking Adventures International and Jedson's Camp . Gear Boots Etc. Including Volks-Ware Other Links Walkn' Walrus Trail Books Trail Videos MapStore Trail Chatter: Our bulletin board page. Now with expert responses from Sherpa Expeditions Walking Chat Room 9 pm ET weeknights Walking Bulletin Board Backpacking ...

Frequent Words: 14:hike 13:walk 5:trail 5:book 4:mail 4:board 4:bulletin 4:camp 4:updat 4:homepag 4:chat 3:llama 3:com 3:shoe 3:thei 3:order 2:expert 2:room 2:vacat 2:foot

Source: Outdoor and Camping - _Leisure and Recreation_
Type: Directory **URL:** http://www.teleport.com:80/~walking/hiking.html
Entered: Tue Feb 28 10:31:41 1995 **Indexed:** Thu Jun 24 10:18:34 1999

2. Samoyeds - K9 Web- *Score: 865 - Size: 16039*

Figure 8–2   Galaxy Search for Hiking

YAHOO

Meta Information

URL: *www.yahoo.com/*

Resource Type: World Wide Web site

Use: finding information, software, and people; very useful for both reference and research

Navigation: browse subject hierarchy and lists of What's New, personalize site, check local Yahoos (e.g., Yahoo-NYC, Yahoo-Chicago, etc.)

Scope: broad, with the following top-level categories: Arts & Humanities, Business & Economy, Computers & Internet, Education, Entertainment, Government, Health, News & Media, Recreation & Sports, Reference, Regional, Science, Social Science, Society & Culture

Strengths: most comprehensive, up-to-date Internet information retrieval resource available; fast, powerful search capability

Submissions: *www.yahoo.com/info/suggest/*

Description

Yahoo is the most comprehensive and up to date of the hierarchical subject-oriented directories of pointers to World Wide Web resources, and it is in many ways the great-grandmother of all directories. Descriptive and evaluative information is provided for some of the resources. The links and information about the referenced resources are gathered in two ways. First, users may submit their own URLs and meta information. Second, automated search robots roam the Internet looking for new resources to add to Yahoo. In addition to browsing the subject hierarchy, users can view a list of What's New, What's Cool, What's Popular, or even a list of random links. The search interface permits users to perform Boolean queries on the title, URL, and comments fields. Case-sensitive matching and substring searching are also possible. Limits can be placed on the number of hits to display.

Yahoo has also taken over Four11's White Pages, which became Yahoo's People Search (*http://people.yahoo.com/*).

Evaluation

As one of the most popular, comprehensive, and up-to-date information retrieval sites on the Internet, Yahoo's strengths are clear. Yahoo has an immense database and links are added on a daily basis. The subject-oriented hierarchy provides intellectual access to the resources, and it is complemented by the What's New lists as well as the flexible search interface. Yahoo now offers not only local versions (Yahoo! NYC) but individualized portal pages (My Yahoo!) The combination of powerful computer hardware, a high-speed Internet connection, and a conscious avoidance of oversize graphics makes Yahoo one of the fastest and most reliable services on the Internet. Whether you're conducting research or seeking a quick answer to a reference question, Yahoo is one of the best places to look.

Sample Search

Objective: John hopes to find information about SGML, an international standard for the description of marked-up electronic text.

Using the subject hierarchy, John selects Computers & Internet and then Information & Documents, then Data Formats, and finally SGML. This takes him to a menu of 16 links to SGML-related resources. Brief descriptions are provided for a few of the resources. Using the query capability, John searches for the keyword **SGML** limited to Computers and Internet and gets 87 hits. In addition to information about the SGML language, John finds links to companies that sell SGML-related products and services to and user groups that meet to discuss SGML. Clearly, when attempting a comprehensive search, a combination of browsing and searching is essential.

LIBRARIANS' INDEX TO THE INTERNET

Meta Information

URL:	*www.lii.org/InternetIndex/*
Resource Type:	World Wide Web site
Use:	aimed at public library users, evaluated and annotated by librarians
Navigation:	Boolean, truncation, subject, title
Scope:	top-level categories include Arts, Automobiles, Business, California, Computers, Cultures (World), Current Events, Disabilities, Education, Families, Food, Gay/Lesbian/Bisexual, Geography, Government, Health, History, Images/Graphics/Clip Art, Internet Information, Jobs, Kids, Law, Libraries, Literature, Media, Men, Miscellaneous, Music, Organizations, People, Philosophy, Politics, Recreation, Reference Desk, Religion, Science, Searching the Internet, Seniors, Sports, Surfing the Internet, Travel, Weather, Women
Updates:	daily
Questions:	cleita@sunsite.berkeley.edu

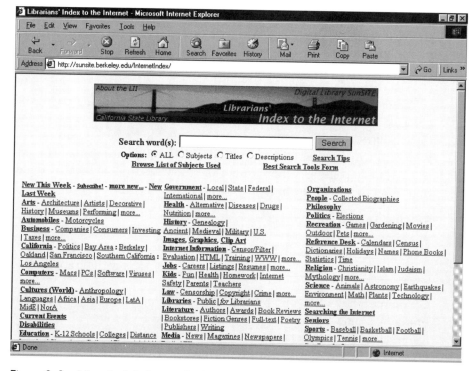

Figure 8–3   Librarian's Index to the Internet *sunsite.berkeley.edu/InternetIndex/>*

Description

Cybrarian Carole Leita created and maintains a splendid index to the Internet; the database is updated daily. Leita will also send subscribers an e-mail listing of some of the best sites added each week; the list is also is maintained at *http://sunsite.berkeley.edu/* and supported in part by Federal Library Services and Technology Act funding, administered by the California State Library (Figure 8–3).

Evaluation

Librarians make their living by connecting people to ideas; this site makes strong descriptive and evaluative connections between people and the information they seek. It is based on the daily work of librarians who do reference work. The list of subjects assigned is included so that people can see categories easily.

When you click on an underlined link from the opening page, you get a clearly organized hierarchy starting with the "Best of" sites on the topic, followed by Directories, Databases, and Specific Resources. For each entry, the name, URL, link, and a description are given. The top of each topic page lists the number of resources to date on that topic. Subcategories under main topics are arranged the same way.

Sample Search

Objective: Giovanna needs to find some information on making her university's Web site accessible to users with disabilities.

Giovanna follows the Disabilities link on the opening page of the Librarians' Guide to the Internet (Figure 8–4). There are 43 resources listed, and under Specific Resources, she finds the following sites: Accessibility Guidelines: Page Authoring (WAI) (*www.w3.org/TR/WD-WAI-PAGEAUTH*), Accessible Web Page Design (*http://weber.u.washington.edu/~doit/Resources/web-design.html*), Bobby: An Automatic Verifier of Web Site Accessibility (*www.cast.org/bobby/*), and Designing a More Useable World (*http://trace.wisc.edu/world/*).

Search Results

There are 43 Internet resources for "disabilities" as of Jul 12, 1999.
To focus your search, select from the term(s) following "Subjects:" under each entry.

Best of ...

Disability Resources Monthly (DRM) - http://www.geocities.com/~drm/
This excellent nonprofit organization Web site provides information about resources for independent living. Major sections are: *DRM WebWatcher*, a selected, annotated guide to disability resources on the Web; *Librarians' Connection*, information about listservs, professional associations, assistive technology and much more; and *Inclusion Resources*, an annotated guide to multicultural, multimedia materials about inclusion and parent advocacy. - cl
Subjects: disabilities |

Directories

Alliance for Technology Access - http://www.ataccess.org/
This is an excellent starting point for information on accessible technology. Their annotated list of Vendors is the most complete and up-to-date I've seen. Their pages on Access to the WWW are great for sorting out what adaptive devices and software aid in access for which disabilities. Also includes great advice on accessible Web page design and links to other technology and disability sites. - cl
Subjects: disabilities |
Blindness Resource Center - http://www.nyise.org/blind.htm
Annotated directory with categories that include: access, braille, deaf-blindness, eye conditions, low vision

Figure 8–4   Disabilities List in Librarians' Index to the Internet

Chapter Nine

Internet Search Tools: A Brief Listing of Places to Start

**Peter Morville, revised
by GraceAnne A. DeCandido**

In the first edition of this book, the distinctions among Internet directories, virtual libraries, and Internet search engines were relatively straightforward. In the few years since then, the distinctions among them have blurred, the relationships among them have become very fluid, as they have merged and taken over from one another, and their opening pages and structure sometimes have little to distinguish them. The meta information is also very fluid.

In Chapter One, Search Engine Watch is discussed as a basic place to start searching or to search about searching. Chapter Two talks about Deja.com for searching newsgroups and Liszt for finding online discussion groups. Chapter Eight talks about Yahoo and other Internet directories. In this chapter, we will look at some search engine sites. It is often difficult to distinguish among these search engines when you are on their opening pages: with banner ads, news headlines, and lists of subjects, as well as the ability of many to tailor or "personalize" the page to the reader's interests, they look more and more alike. In the annotations for the search engines discussed, we will offer distinguishing keys, when available, among these search engines.

People pick a favorite place to start searching and often stick with it, and many librarians prefer to start with Yahoo or with AltaVista. Many users become very attached to a particular search tool, and all of the major ones have their partisans. A trial search can be the best way to see what works for you; even more so, your comfort level with the look and feel of the site (though more and more they resemble one another) or with the ways you can personalize your page will make the difference. Search sites are very fluid; they change often, and often they change to look and behave more like one another than not. Most have banner ads and buttons to places that will sell you things, and most permit you to personalize the opening page to put your interests first. In return, they collect some information about you that is useful for their advertisers.

Internet searching tools constitute the richest and most varied category of resources for finding information, software, people, and communities of people on the Internet. The primary shared characteristic of these tools is the provision of keyword searching capabilities, in contrast to the emphasis placed on the browsing of hierarchical topic trees that we have seen in the virtual libraries and Internet directories. These keyword searching capabilities vary from tool to tool. Some provide only basic full-text searching while others allow for the complex nesting of Boolean queries with support for proximity and adjacency searching. Tools such as Lycos make use of software robots or "spiders" that roam the World Wide Web, indexing the full text of everything they find. Other tools are more specific in nature, helping users to locate and download public domain software, find contact information such as e-mail addresses and phone numbers of individuals, or locate and communicate with communities of people on a particular topic of interest.

Internet search tools are most useful when you are conducting extensive research into a particular topic. When you're looking for Internet information resources, tools in this category typically allow for the most comprehensive searches. Through the use of automated software robots, powerful indexing tools, and advanced search engines, these tools are able to provide access to very large collections. The indexes of some of the best tools contain the full text of millions of World Wide Web documents. Flexible query interfaces provide the user with the ability to perform complex queries on these extensive document databases.

This research orientation is true, with the exception of the tools for finding people and communities of people. Those tools tend to serve more of a reference function. Their strength lies in the provision of fast and easy access to white page directories of individuals and collections of online discussion groups.

The primary weakness of Internet search tools arises from their dependence on automated procedures for indexing, organizing, and presenting information. The lack of editorial control over their indexes leads to collections that vary widely with respect to quality, currency, and type of content. A search on the word **chemistry** may return a list of hits that includes an out-of-date periodic table, a very useful guide to chemistry-related resources on the Internet, and a full listing of the chemistry course offerings at a university. While recall may be high, precision tends to be fairly low.

The tools for finding people and communities of people are different in this respect. These tools typically provide access to well-structured databases of information. Their weaknesses often lie more in the relatively small size of these databases. They are usually far from comprehensive.

SEARCHING TIPS

Since many of these tools provide a unique way to search a unique collection of information, it's very difficult to formulate any general searching strategy. With each tool, the best path to conducting effective queries is through trial and error. Read the searching instructions, try a few searches, and learn from the results.

CONSIDERATIONS FOR THE FUTURE

The evolution of Internet search tools is blazing ahead at an astonishing rate. In a few short years, we've moved from an environment with a couple of very basic tools called Archie and Veronica (now pretty much consigned to the cyberdustbin) to a world where just choosing the right search tool for your purposes is a challenge in itself. Some of today's leading search tools employ intelligent software agents to scour the Internet for information (see Chapter Four), and make use of powerful query interfaces and search engines to provide users with access to these immense bodies of information. However, the rapid advances in this tool set are constantly being challenged by the exponential growth in the amount of Internet information. This growth will place a higher burden on the user who may need to employ the full range of Boolean operators and proximity and adjacency capabilities in order to conduct efficient and effective searches.

There is, however, considerable discussion in the academic world of information science on the uses and future of Boolean searching. This scholarly community tends to be more and more divided on the subject, with some dismissing Boolean outright as outmoded, and others seeing Boolean operators as ripe for continuance in searching the Internet.

Another response to this problem will be increased human involvement in the identification, selection, description, evaluation, and organization of resources that make up these immense global databases of information. As the global information database continues to grow, people will place an increasingly higher value on services that facilitate fast and easy intellectual access to the information they need.

STARTING HERE

The following search engines (listed in alphabetical order) are places to start. Treat the descriptions like a menu of services, and see what works for you. Each description includes information on what sets that particular search engine apart from the others. This is the most interactive section of this book, because you can sit at your computer and try out these services. All URLs are listed in Appendix starting on page 155 and on the Neal-Schuman Web site at *neal-schuman.com/ish.html*.

To complement the following descriptions an excellent Search Tools Chart is available at *http://infopeople.org/src/chart.html*. Created by Carole Leita of the Librarians' Guide to the Internet, it covers selected Internet subject directories and selected search engines.

ALTAVISTA

Meta Information

URL: *www.altavista.com/*

Use: search engine for Web pages and Usenet postings

Navigation: categories, word or phrase, natural language (asking a question as you would phrase it to a friend or colleague)

Scope: top-level categories include Automotive, Business & Finance, Computers & Internet, Health & Fitness, Hobbies & Interests, Home & Family, Media & Amusements, People & Chat, Reference & Education, Shopping & Services, Society & Politics, Sports & Recreation, Travel & Vacations

Volume: full text of 130 million Web pages plus Usenet postings

Questions: search-support@altavista.com

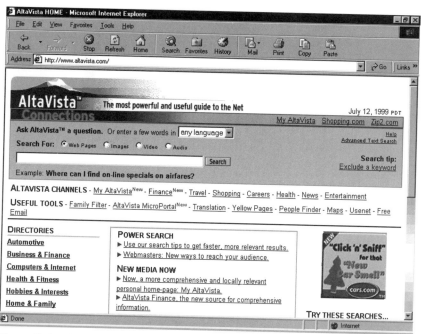

Figure 9–1   AltaVista Opening Page

Description

A great-grandmother of search engines and extremely popular, AltaVista has recently added natural language to its arsenal of searching mechanisms along with Boolean, truncation, and case sensitivity. Searches can be limited by language and date, and various user preferences.

Special Features

AltaVista (Figure 9–1) also offers AV Photo & Media Finder, which enables searches of images and audio files, at *http://image.altavista.com/ cgi-bin/avncgi.*

ASK JEEVES

Meta Information

URL:	*www.askjeeves.com/*
Use:	search engine
Navigation:	natural language (asking a question as you would phrase it to a friend or colleague)
Volume:	150 million questions asked; database of 7 million answers, as of 4/99
Questions:	jeeves@ask.com

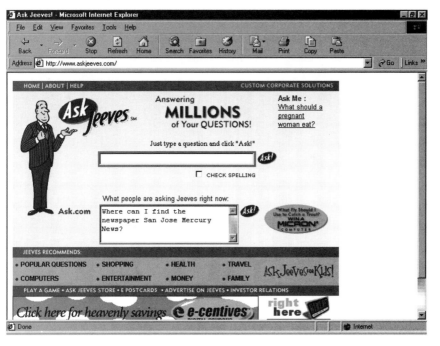

Figure 9–2   Ask Jeeves Opening Page

Description

Ask Jeeves can actually be described as charming: its natural language capability allows users to type in a query as if they were asking a person the question (Figure 9–2). Ask Jeeves will even check your spelling. It has a large database of information, and it also uses other search engines to respond to queries. All of this is invisible, so getting the end result can be rather more fun than average.

Special Features

While you wait for an answer, you can watch other queries flash up on your screen from other Ask Jeeves seekers. A section includes the most popular questions from the previous month. It also has a special section for young people, called Ask Jeeves for Kids (*www.ajkids.com/*).

DOGPILE

Meta Information

URL: *www.dogpile.com/*

Use: a meta-search engine

Navigation: Boolean, quotation marks for phrases

Scope: **The Web**: LookSmart, GoTo.com, Thunderstone, Yahoo!, Dogpile Open Directory, About.com, Lycos' Top 5%, InfoSeek, Direct Hit, Lycos & AltaVista **Usenet**: Reference, Dejanews, AltaVista and Dejanews' old Database. Yahoo News Headlines and Infoseek NewsWires.

Volume: 25 search engines, searched three at a time

Questions: webmaster@dogpile.com

Description

Dogpile searches the Web, Usenet, FTP, weather, stock quotes, and other information you might want to "fetch." Searches can be customized, there's syntax help, and a link to MetaFind.com.

Special Features

Dogpile is a meta-search engine; it searches 25 Web, Usenet, and news search engines, three at a time. You can customize the order of the databases, or eliminate some.

EXCITE

Meta Information

URL:	*www.excite.com*
Use:	search engine
Navigation:	keywords, Boolean, no truncation
Scope:	opening page includes 18 subjects (from Autos to Health to Travel), News, Stocks, Weather, Chat, and Today on Excite
Volume:	keywords of 60 million Web pages, including most archived mailing lists
Questions:	online form for queries

Description

Excite's strength is in conceptual searching, connecting keywords to get to what you want. Its opening page (Figure 9–3) offers a lot of information over a broad spectrum: subject listings, news, stocks, weather, chat, sports, horoscopes. All of this can be personalized to make a page specific to the reader's interests, with information remembered from visit to visit. It maintains member services and a member directory of those who choose to sign in.

Special Features

Excite offers Search Wizard, which suggests words related to the subject you are searching for, activated by a check box. Results can be grouped. Excite includes News Channel (which searches over 300 magazines and newspapers), Travel Channel, and over 25,000 reviews.

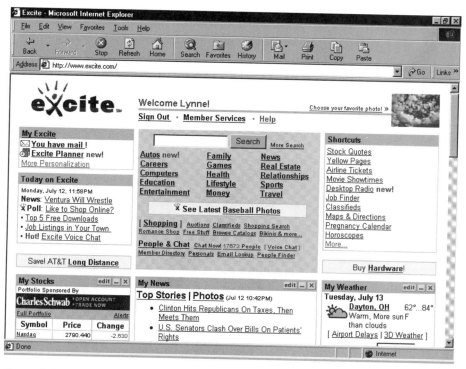

Figure 9–3   Excite Opening Page

HOTBOT

Meta Information

URL: *www.hotbot.com*

Use: search engine "powered by Direct Hit" (according to Hotbot Web site), which ranks results by popularity

Navigation: Boolean, quotation marks for phrases, advanced search; can limit in many ways (such as language, date); can search by media type for pages using specific technologies (such as audio, JavaScript)

Scope: opening page lists four sections: (Stay Informed, Use Technology, Plan a Purchase, Enrich your Life), subsections under each

Volume: full text of 110 million Web pages, including most archived mailing lists

Questions: wow@wired.com

Description

HotBot, part of the Wired Digital group, uses Direct Hit as its default search engine. Direct Hit ranks its results by user popularity, displaying those that are most frequently visited first. Its opening page (Figure 9–4) has the neon but memorable graphics associated with *Wired* magazine and the HotWired Web site, and maintains a look and feel rather different from the increasingly homogenized search engine look.

Special Features

Besides Direct Hit's ranking by popularity, HotBot also permits searching for image, video, JavaScript, and other technologies under its Pages Must Include button.

Figure 9–4   Hotbot Opening Page

INFOSEEK

Meta Information

URL:	*http://infoseek.go.com/*
Use:	search engine
Navigation:	Boolean: AND or OR default; no truncation, case sensitive
Scope:	opening page includes News, Money, Weather, as well as subjects: Automotive, Business, Careers, Computing, Communications, Entertainment, Family, Food and Drink, Games, Health, Kids, Money, News, Real Estate, Shopping, Sports, Travel, Women
Volume:	full text of 45 million Web pages, and Usenet groups from deja.com.
Questions:	comments@infoseek.com

Description

Infoseek is an Internet search tool that allows users to query relatively comprehensive databases of Web pages and Usenet news postings. Complex searches can be constructed using Boolean logic and nested queries. Date ranges may also be specified. Results are presented as a list of hyperlinked titles with brief descriptions that are pulled from the resources themselves. Like many portal sites, Infoseek permits personalization of its opening page after a reader registers (Figure 9–5).

Special Features

Under its Advanced Search option, Infoseek searches such sources as yellow pages, shareware, maps, and dictionary.

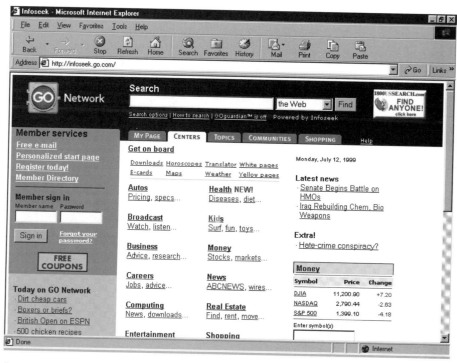

Figure 9–5   Infoseek Opening Page

LYCOS

Meta Information

URL: *www.lycos.com*

Use: search engine

Navigation: Boolean, quotation marks for phrase, no truncation; can search by type of file

Scope: headline news, Featured on Lycos, personalization options; opening page topics include Arts & Entertainment, Business & Careers, Computers & Internet, Games, Health, Home & Family, News, Recreation, Reference, Region, Science & Technology, Shopping, Society & Culture, Sports

Volume: full text of 50 million Web pages, including many archived mailing lists; includes Gopher and FTP sites

Questions: includes online form for questions; also includes corporate address and telephone number (a rarity)

Description

Lycos is an oldie that has gone through many permutations. Now it permits personalization of the opening page (Figure 9–6) after a reader registers. Its advanced search provides the option of searching for a picture, sound, or graphic.

Special Features

Lycos includes a city guide, searchable by continent; a best-of-the-Web, Top 5% of rated sites; and Pictures and Sounds (*www.lycos.com/picturethis/*), available under its advanced search option. Pictures and Sounds enables both Lycos and Web-wide searches.

Figure 9–6   Lycos Opening Page

NORTHERN LIGHT

Meta Information

URL: *www.northernlight.com*

Use: search engine

Navigation: Boolean, quotation marks for phrase; can limit by date and language; results sorted by subject folder

Scope: opening page includes both Web searching and the fee-based Special Collection search, as well as What's New Special Edition and Current News, which are free

Volume: full text of 130 million Web pages; includes fee-based database of 5,400 print resources

Questions: content@nlsearch.com

Description

Northern Light is an engine that combines free Web searching with fee-based searches, which is clearly indicated. Its fee-based Special Collection charges only for what is actually read. Summaries of articles are free; documents are available instantly after secure online credit card transactions (Figure 9–7).

Special Features

Northern Light groups its search results into subject folders, which is very handy for retrieval. Its Current News (for the past two weeks) and Special Edition for in-depth news are very useful.

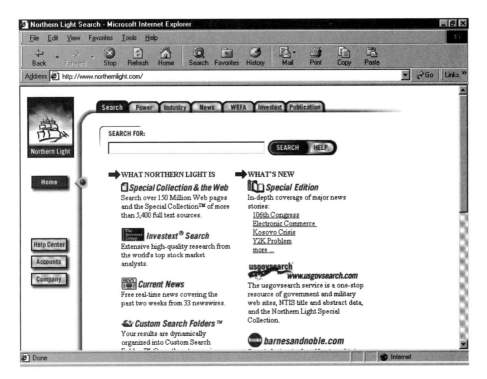

Figure 9–7   Northern Light Opening Page

OTHER SITES WITH HANDY TOOLS

Some of the following tools are new, some not. All of them provide something not easily found in other tools, and thus they are definitely worth a visit.

Google

Besides its way-cool name, one of Google's (*www.google.com/*) advantages is that it operates on the principle that links of high importance/authority linked to the page you are searching for will give quality results, and they use that in their queries (Figure 9–8). They also provide an I'm Feeling Lucky button, which will take you directly to the Web page that is the top result of your search rather than to a list of possible links.

Figure 9–8   Google Opening Page

Metacrawler

Metacrawler (*www.metacrawler.com*) searches AltaVista, Excite, Infoseek, Lycos, Thunderstone, WebCrawler, and Yahoo. It has a nifty feature called MetaSpy (*www.metaspy.com/*), which enables you to see the searches being performed on Metacrawler in real time, and which refreshes itself every 15 seconds (Figure 9–9).

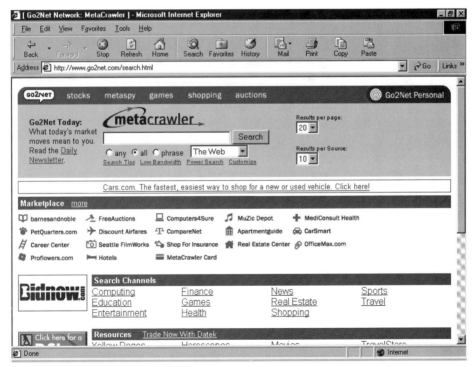

Figure 9–9   Metacrawler Opening Page

Inter-Links

Inter-Links (*http://alabanza.com/kabacoff/Inter-Links/*) is a refreshing change because it has no banners or advertising (Figure 9–10). It functions as an Internet navigator, resource locator, and tutorial.

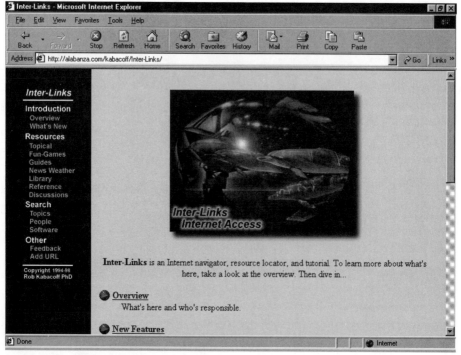

Figure 9–10   Inter-Links Opening Page

InferenceFind

InferenceFind (*www.infind.com/*) calls WebCrawler, Yahoo, Lycos, AltaVista, InfoSeek, and Excite, and then groups the results by type (for example, all of the *.edu* sites are listed together), or all of the sites from a particular country (Figure 9–11).

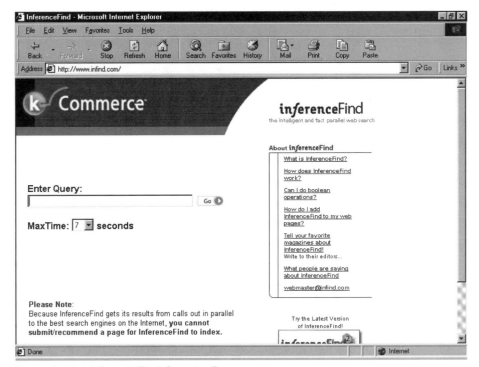

Figure 9–11   InferenceFind Opening Page

SEARCHING FOR FAQ OR MAILING LIST INFORMATION

FAQ Archives

FAQ archives (*www.cs.ruu.nl/cgi-bin/faqwais*) is a neat archive of FAQs posted in the Usenet newsgroup news.answers (Figure 9–12). It comes from the University of Utrecht Department of Computer Science.

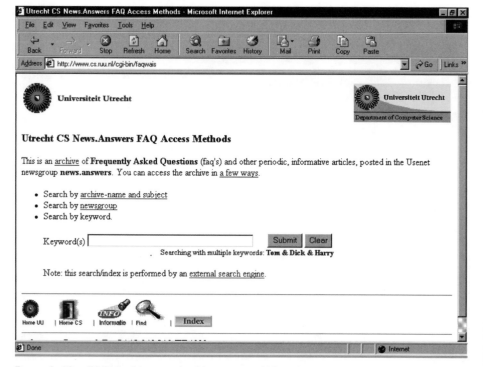

Figure 9–12   FAQ Archives at the University of Utrecht

PAML

PAML: Publicly Accessible Mailing Lists (*www.NeoSoft.com:80/internet/ paml/*) answers the eternal question, how do I unsubscribe? Offering a quick history of PAML's growth and development, current managers Stephanie and Peter da Silva post updates once a month to the Usenet usegroups news.lists.misc and news.answers. The new version always supersedes the old, and the Usenet version is the definitive copy (Figure 9–13).

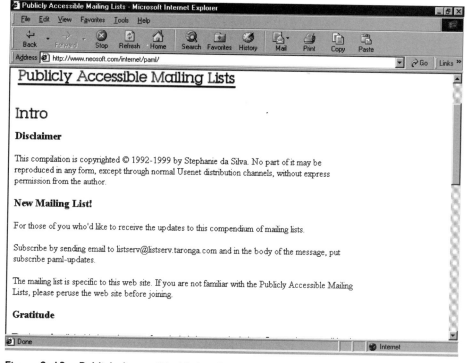

Figure 9–13   Publicly Accessible Mailing Lists Opening Page

Liszt (*www.liszt.com*), described in Chapter Two lists online discussions.

Directory of Scholarly and Professional E-Conferences

The Directory of Scholarly and Professional E-Conferences (*http:// n2h2.com/KOVACS/*) is a database of electronic mailing lists and Usenet newsgroups of a scholarly nature (Figure 9–14). The print and Web publication, now in its 13th revision, is published by the Association of Research Libraries. Send questions to Diane Kovacs, diane@kovacs.com.

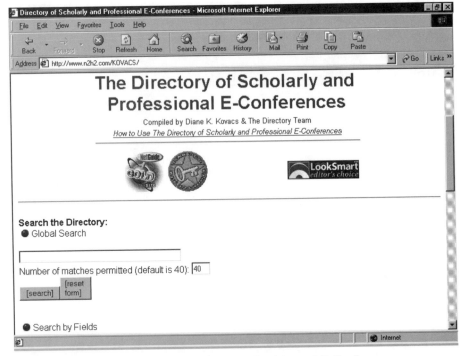

Figure 9–14   The Directory of Scholarly and Professional E-Conferences

Chapter Ten

Web Rings, GIS, and a Few Closing Thoughts

GraceAnne A. DeCandido

If you have been wandering around the chapters of this book, or following them more or less in order, you now have a pretty good idea how to find things on the Internet. This last chapter mentions a few things that you should know about but that didn't fit any place else, and shares a few thoughts on the future (which probably means, oh, next week or so).

WEB RINGS

Web rings are a more homespun feature of the Internet: essentially, a Web ring is a group of related sites linked to each other via computer code, so that using the Back or Forward buttons, or a random button, will bring the user to the next site in the ring. Some Web rings are circular, so you end up back where you began; others run straight through the sites. A Web ring by its nature and design is focused on a single topic, so it is a manageable alternative to search engine glut. Web rings are an attractive alternative to the ubiquitous list of favorite links. Web rings are connected by subject and by the code that loops them together.

Web rings were invented by Sage Weil, who wrote the CGI script that hold Web rings together, when he was in high school in Ashland, Oregon, in 1995. There are now more than 60,000 Web rings, searchable at *webring.org*, now owned by Geocities (Figure 10–1).

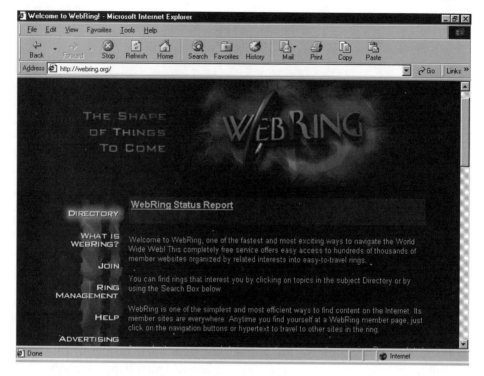

Figure 10–1 Webring.org Opening Page

Web ring subjects are as far-ranging as anything on the Net, from science fiction to knitting. There is a lot of web ring history at webring.org, as well as a nifty directory, which is the easiest way to locate a particular Web ring. The lure and lore of Web rings was brought to the editor's attention by an article in the *New York Times* Circuits section, G1, January 21, 1999, "Surfing in Circles and Loving It," written by Tina Kelley; and by Carol Casey's article "Web Rings: An Alternative to Search Engines" in *College and Research Library News*, November 1998, 761–763.

GIS

Geographic (or Geospatial) Information Systems, or GIS, is another way of finding information by adding a spatial dimension to problem solving. We are including GIS in this guide for three reasons:

- It represents an excellent example of how the yoking of hardware, software, and data can be used by people to find things and solve problems in entirely new ways.

- It represents a kind of information gathering that was previously impossible without Net access.
- It models the kind of creative synergy that Net searching facilitates.

GIS enables users to see spatial connections. To use an example from George Soete's ARL Transforming Libraries #2, *Issues and Innovations in Geographic Information Systems*, February 1997, GIS can layer the locations of public health clinics, city bus lines, and residents who fall below the poverty line in income. This capability enables urban planners to make decisions about changing bus routes, requesting funding, or other kinds of crucial public health issues.

GIS grew up from the availability in the 1990s of such government data as census information in machine-readable form, and the availability of software to layer the data. Good basic information about GIS is available on the following Web sites:

A Guide to GIS Resources on the Internet
http://sunsite.berkeley.edu/~smorris/gisnet.html

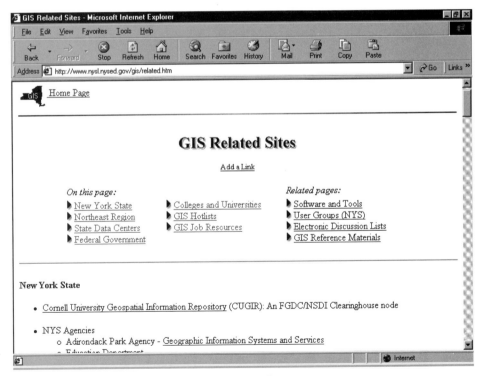

Figure 10–2 New York State's GIS Related Sites Page

Census TIGER 1995 Data
www.esri.com/data/online/tiger/
TIGER is Topologically Integrated Geographic Encoding and Referencing, a digital database of geographic features (such as roads, railroads, rivers, lakes, political boundaries, census statistical boundaries), covering the entire United States.

New York State's GIS Related Sites (Figure 10–2)
www.nysl.nysed.gov/gis/related.htm
Contains many links to GIS sites across the country.

BUT IS WHAT YOU FOUND ANY GOOD?

It is beyond the scope and focus of this book to analyze how you ascertain whether the stuff you have found on the Web is actually worth it. There are, however, numerous sites and a new Neal-Schuman title that will help you do just that. Cybrarian-writer Carolyn Caywood has an excellent site (*www6.pilot.infi.net/~carolyn/criteria.html*), called Library Selection Criteria for WWW Resources (Figure 10–3), that is not only good and clear, but also links to other such sites. You will also find lots of good advice at *www.neal-schuman.com/ish*.

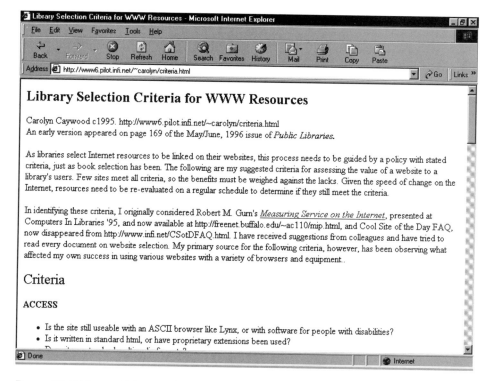

Figure 10–3 Library Selection Criteria for WWW Resources

IT'S NEVER THE LAST WORD

In the months we have worked on this book, some things we wrote in November have been made untrue by January; and new stuff in January was old stuff by May. The changes since the first edition are enormous. URLs fill advertisements and business cards; just as one company seeks to find another way to make money off the Net, another maverick provides a free source or a different way of looking for what we want to find. The metaphors for the Net proliferate: it's a jungle, it's an ocean, it's a flea market, it's a mess. But there are other metaphors. Like the late, beloved Paul Evan Peters' vision of the Net as a kind of hunter-gatherer society, where some folks never leave their own valley (or search engine) while others can't wait to see what is over the next URL. Or a metaphor I used in an editorial in the late, lamented *Wilson Library Bulletin* when I was its editor-in-chief: the Internet as Venice. In the May 1993 "Brazen Overtures" editorial page, I wrote:

> The Internet is like Venice. Everything is unexpected, the buses ride on the water, getting from here to there is a leap of faith. But everywhere you go there is something worth looking at, even though it is not what your poorly translated guidebook was leading you to (p. 8).

Like Joe Janes in Chapter One, we can be astonished by how quaint information about the Net that is only a few years old can sound. Like Sara Ryan in Chapter Two, we note that the level of sophistication of Net users, even beginning ones, has deepened greatly. About the only things we can feel confident predicting are that change will happen more rapidly than we expect, and that it may move in directions that we can't quite see on the horizon yet.

We shape our tools, and are shaped by them, to paraphrase Marshall McLuhan. Our usage shapes the Net, and the Net shapes our searches with its wanton ways. Cyberspace can be a rich and beguiling source. And we, by what we seek and what we find, make it so.

Appendix

Find It Quick: Sites Featured in
The Internet Searcher's Handbook

Foreword

H. W. Wilson
www.hwwilson.com/history.html

Argus Associates
http://argus-inc.com

Ask Jeeves
www.askjeeves.com/

Chapter One

Parliamentary and Presidential Elections Around the World
www.agora.stm.it/elections/election.htm

Internet Movie Database
http://us.imdb.com

Search Engine Watch
www.searchenginewatch.com/

American Library Association
www.ala.org

The White House
www.whitehouse.gov

Biography (television)
www.biography.com

The New York Times
www.nytimes.com

Amnesty International
www.amnesty.org

Northwest Airlines
www.nwa.com

The State of Michigan
www.state.mi.us

Argus Clearinghouse
www.clearinghouse.net

Internet Public Library
www.ipl.org

Yahoo
www.yahoo.com

AltaVista
www.altavista.com

Hotbot
www.hotbot.com

Excite
www.excite.com

Metacrawler
www.metacrawler.com

Chapter Two

Paper presented at the Internet Society 1998 Annual Meeting
www.caida.org/Papers/Inet98/

Plotnikoff's *San José Mercury News* column
www.mercurycenter.com/columnists/plotnikoff/docs/dp101898.htm

List of country code
www.iana.org/country-codes.txt

Whatis.com
www.whatis.com/

Ask A+ Locator/ERIC
www.vrd.org/locator/

Deja.com
www.deja.com/

Liszt
www.liszt.com/

Librarians' lists
www.wrlc.org/liblists//liblists.htm

Web4Lib Archives
http://sunsite.berkeley.edu/Web4Lib/archive.html

Chapter Three

Metadata schemes
www.w3.org/Metadata/
http://purl.org/dc/about/element_set.htm

Visual Arts Data Service
http://vads.ahds.ac.uk

Dublin Core
http://purl.org/dc/about/elements/1.1

Cover, Robin, SGML/XML Applications: Government, Military, and Heavy Industry
www.oasis-open.org/cover/gov-apps.html

Cover, Robin, SGML/XML Academic Applications
www.oasis-open.org/cover/acadapps.html

Finding Aids online
http://sunsite.berkeley.edu/FindingAids/findaids.html
http://digilib.nypl.org/dynaWeb/dhc/findaid/@Generic__CollectionView

Text Encoding Initiative (TEI) DTD
www-tei.uic.edu/orgs/tei/info/hist.html

Applications using TEI
www-tei.uic.edu/orgs/tei/app/index.html

NYPL's Digital Schomburg African-American Women Writers of the 19th
Century
http://digital.nypl.org/schomburg/writers_aa19/

The University of Virginia Modern English Collection
http://etext.virginia.edu/etcbin/ot2www-eng2?specfile=/lv4/modeng/www/
modeng-pub.o2w

Chapter Four

Jango
http://jango.excite.com/xsh/index.dcg?

Newshound
www.newshound.com/

Linkbot
www.tetranetsoftware.com/products/linkbot.htm (This site also links to
freeware Linkbot Express.)

Robot Exclusion Standards
http://info.webcrawler.com/mak/projects/robots/norobots.html#status

Dr. Clue's HTML guide
www.drclue.net/

MS Agent
www.microsoft.com/workshop/imedia/agent/agentdl.asp

Argolink
www.argolink.com/

Intelligent Agents Project at IBM T. J. Watson Research
www.research.ibm.com/iagents/ibm

The Botspot
www.botspot.com

Links 2 Go
www.links2go.com/topic/Agents

Chapter Five

Lycos
www.lycos.com

Argus Clearinghouse list on ecology
*www.clearinghouse.net/cgi-bin/chadmin/viewcat/Environment/
ecology?kywd++*

Yahoo
www.yahoo.com

Ask Jeeves
www.askjeeves.com

Publicly Accessible Mailing Lists (PAML)
www.NeoSoft.com:80-/internet/paml

Liszt
www.liszt.com

Deja.com
www.deja.com

Chapter Six

Stumpers
www.cuis.edu/~stumpers/

Unofficial Stumpers "Womb@t" Page
www.du.edu/~penrosel/wombat/index.html

Chapter Seven

Drudge Report
www.drudgereport.com

Buffy Cross and Stake
http://slayer.simplenet.com/tbcs/main.html

Argus Clearinghouse
www.clearinghouse.net/

Internet Public Library
www.ipl.org/

Magellan
http://magellan.excite.com/

World Wide Web Virtual Library
http://vlib.org/Overview.html

Genealogy Home Page
www.genhomepage.com

Beer Info Source
www.beerinfo.com/vlib/index.html

About.com
www.about.com/

Chapter Eight

Galaxy
www.einet.net/ or *www.galaxy.com*

Hiking Resources
www.gorp.com:80/gorp/activity/hiking.htm

Yahoo
www.yahoo.com

Yahoo's People Search
http://people.yahoo.com/

Librarians' Index to the Internet
http://sunsite.berkeley.edu/InternetIndex/
or
www.lii.org/InternetIndex/

Accessibility Guidelines: Page Authoring (WAI)
www.w3.org/TR/WD-WAI-PAGEAUTH

Accessible Web Page Design
http://weber.u.washington.edu/~doit/Resources/web-design.html

Bobby: An Automatic Verifier of Web Site Accessibility
www.cast.org/bobby/

Designing a More Useable World
http://trace.wisc.edu/world/

Chapter Nine

Deja.com
www.deja.com/

Search Tools Chart
http://infopeople.org/src/chart.html

AltaVista
www.altavista.com/

AV Photo and Image Finder
http://image.altavista.com/cgi-bin/avncgi

Ask Jeeves
www.askjeeves.com/

Ask Jeeves for Kids
www.ajkids.com/

Dogpile
www.dogpile.com/

Excite
www.excite.com

HotBot
www.hotbot.com

InfoSeek
www.infoseek.go.com/

Lycos
www.lycos.com/

Pictures & Sounds
www.lycos.com/picturesthis/

Northern Light
www.northernlight.com

Google
www.google.com/

Metacrawler
www.metacrawler.com

Metapsy
www.metaspy.com

Inter-Links
http://alabanza.com/kabacoff/Inter-Links/

InferenceFind
www.infind.com/

FAQ archives
www.cs.ruu.nl/cgi-bin/faqwais

PAML: Publicly Accessible Mailing Lists
www.NeoSoft.com:80/internet/paml/

Liszt
www.liszt.com/

Directory of Scholarly and Professional E-Conferences
http://n2h2.com/KOVACS/

Chapter Ten

Web rings
http://webring.org/

A Guide to GIS Resources on the Internet
http://sunsite.berkeley.edu/~smorris/gisnet.html

Census Tiger 1995 Data
www.esri.com/data/online/tiger/

New York State's GIS Related Sites
www.nysl.nysed.gov/gis/related.htm

Library Selection Criteria for WWW Resources
www6.pilot.infi.net/~carolyn/criteria.html

About the Contributors

GraceAnne A. DeCandido, M.L.S., is a writer, teacher, speaker, and consultant in her own company, Blue Roses Editorial and Web Consulting (*www.well.com/user/ladyhawk/gadhome.html*), in New York City. She has worked in public, academic, and special libraries, and held editorial posts at *Library Journal* and *School Library Journal* before becoming Editor in chief of the late, lamented *Wilson Library Bulletin*. She has written papers, documents, and Web pages for many divisions of the American Library Association, for the Reader's Digest Foundation Tall Tree Initiative for Schools and Libraries in Westchester County, N.Y., and for the Association of Research Libraries, among many others. She has been a book reviewer for 25 years, most recently for *Booklist* and for *Kirkus Reviews*. She's been married for over 30 years to Robert DeCandido (see below), and is the Mom to Keith R. A. DeCandido, author of Spider-man, Young Hercules, and Buffy, the Vampire Slayer novels. She can be reached via e-mail at ladyhawk@well.com.

Robert DeCandido is a specialist in digitizing and preservation at the New York Public Library (NYPL); he has been with the Preservation Division of NYPL since 1974. He has helped develop a number of web resources for that institution's Research Libraries, including African-American Women Writers of the 19th Century (an SGML transcription of 41 works), Images of African-Americans from the 19th Century (an indexed collection of over 500 images), and Archival Finding Aids of The New York Public Library (a growing collection of SGML descriptions of archival collections). He is currently working on several digital projects in the performing arts, New York State history, and the history of transportation in America. He can be reached via e-mail at rdecandido@ nypl.org.

Joseph Janes is at the School of Library and Information Science at the University of Washington and is founding director of the Internet Public Library. A frequent speaker in the United States and abroad, he is the coauthor of seven books on librarianship and technology, including the *Internet Public Library Handbook* (Neal-Schuman, 1999). He holds M.L.S. and Ph.D. degrees from Syracuse University, and has taught at the University of Michigan, the University of North Carolina at Chapel Hill, the University at Albany, the State University of New York, as well as at Syracuse and Washington. He can be reached via e-mail at jwj@u.washington.edu.

Peter Morville is vice president of Argus Associates (*http://argus-inc.com/*), an information architecture consulting firm based in Ann Arbor, Michigan. Morville is coauthor of *Information Architecture for the World Wide Web* (O'Reilly, 1998), a regular contributor to *Web Review* magazine, and a frequent speaker at numerous trade shows and conferences. Peter holdsan M.I.L.S. from the University of Michigan and a B.A. in English literature from Tufts University. Argus Associates provides information architecture consulting services to such corporate clients as AT&T, Barron's, Borders, Chrysler, Compaq, Dow Chemical, Goodyear, Johnson & Johnson, and UMI. Argus is unusual since it is staffed by entrepreneurial librarians who apply the principles of their profession in new online environments where they're desperately needed. Peter Morville can be reached via e-mail at morville@argus-inc.com.

Lou Rosenfeld is president and co-founder of Argus Associates, an information architecture consulting firm that has been a pioneer in transporting the principles of information retrieval and librarianship to the Web. Rosenfeld is coauthor of *Information Architecture for the World Wide Web* (O'Reilly, 1998), a regular contributor to *Internet World* and *Web Review* magazines, and a frequent speaker at numerous trade shows and conferences. Argus Associates provides information architecture consulting services to such corporate clients as AT&T, Barron's, Borders, Chrysler, Compaq, Dow Chemical, Goodyear, Johnson & Johnson, and UMI. He can be reached via e-mail at lou@argus-inc.com.

Sara Ryan is a librarian with the Multnomah County Library School Corps in Portland, Oregon. The School Corps is a library outreach program that works directly with teachers, students, and media specialists in K–12 public and private schools in Multnomah County to provide training on the efficient and effective use of public library resources, particularly electronic resources. Ryan is coauthor of *The Internet Public Library Handbook* (Neal-Schuman, 1999). She can be reached via e-mail at sryan@nethost.multnomah.lib.or.us. Copyright © 1999 by Sara Ryan.

Steve Ruddy is Web coordinator of the New York Public Library (Research Libraries), and he says, "Information architecture and Web strategy designed to bring libraries into the world of the new Web—that is what I'm thinking about all day. Pet projects include getting an online art gallery up before the year 2000, creating a metadata search engine for research institutions, and one day actually having an intelligent library agent based on the librarian from Neal Stephenson's *Snowcrash* to do all of my work for me." He can be reached via e-mail at sruddy@nypl.org.

Stephanie Walker is the director of Directory Services for Galaxy (*www.galaxy.com/*) and HealthWave (*www.healthwave.com/*) at America's Health Network in Austin, Texas. Stephanie has a B.A. in English from the University of Southern Mississippi and an M.L.I.S. from the Graduate School of Library and Information Science at the University of Texas at Austin. She also created the subject hierarchy for DejaNews now Deja.com (*www.deja.com*) in which she categorized 10,000 Usenet newsgroups. She can be reached via e-mail at swalker@galaxy.com. Copyright © 1999 by Stephanie Walker.

W. Frederick Zimmerman is editor and publisher of the Internet Book Information Center (*www.internetbookinfo.com*). He can be reached via e-mail at ibic@internetbookinfo.com. Copyright © 1999 by W. Frederick Zimmerman.

Index

Page numbers in bold indicate a page with a figure.